T0171484

Reclaiming Our Children

Pamela Davidson

WESTBOW
PRESS
A DIVISION OF THOMAS NELSON

WestBow Press books may be ordered through booksellers or by contacting:

WestBow Press
A Division of Thomas Nelson
1663 Liberty Drive
Bloomington, IN 47403
www.westbowpress.com
1-(866) 928-1240

ISBN: 978-1-4497-6295-7 (e)
ISBN: 978-1-4497-6296-4 (sc)
ISBN: 978-1-4497-6297-1 (hc)

Library of Congress Control Number: 2012914516

Printed in the United States of America

WestBow Press rev. date: 9/14/2012

To my three good and perfect gifts, Rachel Kathleen,
Julia Patrice, and Spencer Joseph

CONTENTS

PREFACE

Writing this book—any book— was definitely not an idea that originated with me. While I love to read, I can't say that I love to write. Almost everyone knows someone who says that someday they *are* going to write a book. May God help and bless them, but I never included myself among that group.

More than six years ago, a prophetic word from a sister in Christ prompted me to outline what subjects I might want to include in a book—should I ever actually write one. Periodically I wrote a little and thought a lot, convinced this was a spiritual exercise that somehow would strengthen me, but likely would have little benefit for others.

Reasons/excuses abounded for why the manuscript should not become a book. First of all, who but my children would have any interest in my parenting journey? What if they were unpleasantly surprised or embarrassed by something I said? (That wouldn't be a first.)

Reason number two for not becoming a published author is because I am simply an ordinary person. There are no awards or trophies bearing my name. Neither have I held elected office, pastored a church, starred in a film, or done anything to receive headline attention. In other words, I have no name recognition. Why would anyone consider anything I wrote to be worthy of reading?

The third reason is that for me the writing process is laborious and unexciting, so why would I put in the required time and effort, considering the first two reasons?

It was the Holy Spirit who kept nudging me to prepare a manuscript, and He can be very persistent. Every few months my pastor, Dennis

Rouse, poses this question to the Victory World Church congregation. *"What is it that God wants you to do that you haven't done yet?"* Inwardly I would groan and outwardly I would squirm because he was speaking directly to me, and I knew the answer to the question. Finally, I reached the point where my conviction outweighed all my trepidation, and I gave up my procrastination.

My eagerness for putting my parenting story on paper matched my prior eagerness thirty-four years ago for entering the world of parenting. With my first pregnancy, it wasn't the labor and delivery that concerned me. I figured I could physically withstand several hours of pain in order for my baby to safely arrive. It was the next eighteen years that had me worried. I knew I was about as equipped to parent as I would be if I suddenly found myself an astronaut aboard a rocket to the moon. I was entering a whole new world.

Perhaps God wants to encourage you by pointing to me. "Look at my daughter Pam. She knew that without Me, she could do nothing. I empowered and equipped her. I will do no less for any of My children whom I call to be parents."

ACKNOWLEDGEMENTS

There are those who deserve special acknowledgement for their prayer support, friendship, and encouragement during this whole process: Leslie Earle, who kept reminding me to finish what I had started; Linda Hinton and the Women of the Word, who seemed to believe that I actually would; Linda Fritchlee, mentor extraordinaire who goes above and beyond; my husband Jack, who has put up with me for a long time. To all of you, I give sincere gratitude and love.

INTRODUCTION

For dozens of generations, the primary expectation of little girls in America was that one day they would get married, have babies, and rear their sons and daughters to do the same. Even in my lifetime, spinsters were pitied. Today the word "spinster" is nearly obsolete in oral usage. However, the women who were pitied the most were those who were barren. To be married without children was to be only half fulfilled.

Then in the 1960's young women began to rethink the issue. Due to medical advances in reproductive birth control, namely the Pill, women started realizing they could exercise more control over when to have that first baby—and the second baby. And did they really want a third baby?

Concurrently with reproductive rights, the entire movement of women's rights was gaining tremendous momentum. The new feminists were spouting the message that there were no longer "male" jobs that should be performed by men only. No longer should a woman be restricted by the traditional female roles, especially non-paying ones. She should liberate herself! Get free from the drudgery of housework! Get free from the wailing demands of children! With training or education, a woman could do just about any job a man could do, could often do it better, and by golly, her paycheck should equal that of her male counterpart. Anyone who didn't believe that was old fashioned at best and biased against women at worst.

A popular singer of that era, Helen Reddy's lyrics said, "I am woman; hear me roar", and in dens across America, the lionesses were exercising their vocal cords.

"I am going back to work when the baby is six weeks old."

"My job is too important."

"The company needs me."

"I'd go crazy if I stayed home all day."

As a young college grad and new wife, these cultural messages were bombarding me in 1974. In many ways they contrasted with my traditional upbringing where my mother stayed at home raising four children. Four of my aunts chose to become teachers, a perfectly acceptable occupation where women numbered in the majority. When my aunts started having their own children, three of them became fulltime moms. A fifth aunt served as a church secretary, another "female" job.

An integral part of my childhood and teen years revolved around our Baptist church. It was there my parents met as teenagers. My grandparents still attended every Sunday. I was taken to church twice on Sundays and every Wednesday night, and that was fine with me. Accepting Jesus as my Savior and joining the church at age ten, I wanted to be actively involved in everything.

In my early twenties I was exposed to a more contemporary style of worship service and it had a lasting influence. I realized that God was not offended if the pastor and parishioners dressed casually or sang songs that were not in the hymnbook.

Yes, I was a traditionally-raised girl who yearned to be a "hip" woman of the Seventies. My story is how God took me, least likely among my peers to ever be a fulltime mom, on a journey of parenthood that completely convinced me that motherhood is the highest calling there is. What I thought I didn't want to do—what I thought I *couldn't* do— God did through me, and in God-like fashion, *He does all things well.*

1   Parenting Is a Calling

In the vocation of Christian ministry the word "call" has a specialized definition. If a person states he was "called" to preach the gospel, he may be indicating that in his spirit he heard that still small voice speaking to him. Or he may mean that he feels a powerfully strong pull, and believing that the pull is coming from the Holy Spirit, he is compelled to go in a specific direction. The action that follows such a pull is referred to as "answering the call". If you consider yourself a son or daughter of God, then you have answered His call to be a follower.

Have you ever heard someone insist he was "called" to be an engineer or an accountant or a musician? Probably not. Utilizing talents or developing skills to enter an occupation of interest just makes sense to the natural mind, but our spiritual side discounts that. "Called" has been reserved for areas of service that directly further the Kingdom of God here on earth. Translating the Bible into an obscure dialect? Definitely this is a calling. Overseeing the building of a high-rise apartment? This is a job—not a calling.

Yet the construction project manager who is also a disciple of Jesus may be exactly where God can best use him. His work ethic may be raising the performance standard on the site. His prayers may be providing protection from hazards. His humility and fairness may be fostering better teamwork, so that each worker looks out not only for himself, but also for the welfare of all. In essence, the construction project manager's very life gives glory to God and attracts others to the same lifestyle. Who are we to say his career is not also his calling?

In his book *Driven by Eternity,* pastor John Bevere states that when it's all said and done, God will judge us according to what we were *called to do.* That will be His divine measuring stick. It won't matter how many Bibles we passed out on a downtown street corner if what we were *called to do* was to teach the seventh grade boys Sunday school class and we didn't do it.

Now let's apply the "called" concept to the 24/7 job of motherhood. If God is the giver of life, if life begins at conception, and if conception results in a viable human being, then surely God is "calling" someone to take responsibility for meeting the needs of that little life He created. Most of the time it is the biological mother, although there are obvious exceptions.

The fifteen-year-old girl who wanted to try sex is not likely to be well-equipped for such an undertaking. If her family is unwilling or unable to step up and support both her and her baby, then the adoption option may be optimal. Whether the biological mother is able or not, I can say with certainty is that God is calling *someone* to parent that child.

Whether a child is "planned" in the human sense of the term makes no difference. The baby certainly came as no surprise to the Creator. He has known every one of our names since the beginning of time.

Psalm 139:15–16 declares that the Lord sees a baby as it develops in the womb. Before those little eyes have ever seen light, God has determined plans and assigned purposes to His creation. Therefore, the "unplanned" pregnancy must be viewed from a higher perspective.

When a single mother chooses what I have called the "adoption option" above, it is evidence that the God of the universe has not only formed a human life, but He has heard the cries of a childless couple, and now He presents them with a baby. With that gift comes a call to nurture not just physical development, but also spiritual development, so that one day the next generation will be prepared to assume the parental role.

As a bride in 1974, I eagerly embraced a wifely, domestic role—particularly cooking. I also sought my career niche, and somehow landed in the world of casualty insurance claims, a perfect fit with my sociology major. (Yes, there's some sarcasm here.)

What I did not automatically embrace was the idea of having children. As a teen, babysitting was just a way to earn money. Babies didn't make me feel all warm and fuzzy inside. As the eldest child of four, I had experienced just how annoying little kids could be. I was secretly convinced that I just didn't have what it took to be a good mother; therefore, it wouldn't be fair to subject a child to me.

My husband, on the other hand, assumed that one day we'd start a family. Actually, we had never thoroughly discussed the issue, and we'd been married nearly four years. In my mind, it was an "undecided", and because I have a decisive nature, I cannot allow anything to remain undecided for an indeterminate amount of time.

A letter from a college friend who had moved to Taiwan served to bring the issue to the forefront. She wrote that she and her husband had decided that they did not want to have children, and furthermore, he had had a vasectomy.

As the implications sank into my mind, I felt envious. Not envious that my friend's husband had a vasectomy, but that they had reached a decision. I was envious that now she *knew* the path her life would take. She *knew* that there would be no children. As a couple they could make all sorts of other decisions based on that single decision.

They could buy a house and know they wouldn't outgrow it. In choosing a house, they wouldn't have to consider the school district. When they moved from Taiwan, they could live anywhere else in the world they wanted to without regard as to whether it would be a good place to raise a child.

Yes, I was envious, and within a couple weeks the thought that Jack and I needed to determine whether our future would hold babies or not was nearly consuming me. Little did I suspect that it was the Holy Spirit stirring within. Had I ever prayed about this? I don't think so.

All I know is that one evening, I suddenly began crying, and moaning, and hearing the Lord more clearly than I had heard Him in years. He was telling me that He wanted me to be a mother.

This was not what I wanted to hear, and I cried even harder. I even dared to argue, unmindful that God is immutable. After what seemed like hours, (but more likely was closer to fifteen minutes), I stopped crying, stopped arguing and submitted. I replaced "I don't want to" with a reluctant "Okay." I was filled with peace.

Incidentally, this encounter with the Lord did not take occur in the solitude of my home. He chose to grab my attention while my husband and I were sitting by a fountain in a busy outdoor shopping area. Jack was clueless as to why I was having a public breakdown, but after I composed myself, I explained what had transpired. He listened carefully and then asked the obvious question. "When do you want to get pregnant?" *Want* to get pregnant?

Not so fast! I'd just finished telling God that I was *willing* to be a mother, not that I wanted to! Maybe willing obedience was really all God was requiring! If I stopped taking my birth control pills at the end of my current cycle, wouldn't I be demonstrating willing obedience? Maybe He wouldn't actually make me follow through with the whole pregnancy thing. I tried to convince myself this was like summer camp where half the twelve-year-olds stand up when the pastor asks who would go be a missionary in Africa. How many of those kids actually became missionaries? Exactly! God didn't hold them to that! He probably wouldn't hold me to this, for surely He didn't actually expect *me* to have a baby.

However, the Lord had no intention of allowing me to slip out of my agreement. Within a month I had conceived, and following nine months and two weeks of almost daily heartburn, (and a weight gain of more than forty pounds), I gave birth to a beautiful daughter. This was prior to the "have three ultrasounds-find out the sex-and tell the world" era. Until she was finally *ex utero*, I had no idea whether my baby would be a boy or girl, and it didn't make the slightest bit of difference. That day was the beginning of a lifetime love affair with Rachel.

Smart enough to know that I knew nothing about babies, I had tried to educate myself by reading book after book during those nine months. Still, I was a very nervous and inexperienced new mother. My own motherly mother came to my house and stayed with us for a week, and I count that as one of the most special gifts she's ever given me. When it was time for her to leave, she reassured me that I would be able to handle everything on my own. All the while I was resisting the urge to cry, to cling to her, and to beg her not to leave until Rachel went to kindergarten.

All babies are born demanding. (That's the first evidence of the truth that we are born with a sin nature.) They want to eat *now*. They want to be held *now*!

God seemed to be giving me another test by giving me a child who thrived on stimulation and activity. Rachel didn't take real naps. I'm talking about naps that are two to three hours in length during which you can do things like clean the house or prepare a nice dinner. Even I—the teen who didn't like to babysit—didn't need a baby book to tell me that infants were supposed to spend their time eating and sleeping. Rachel did the eating part very well. The sleeping posed a problem.

Miss Rachel seemed to thrive on twenty-minute catnaps. This created the challenge of how to shower, shampoo, shave legs, blow-dry hair, and get dressed in twenty minutes. After a few weeks of what I was sure had to be abnormal behavior on her part, I called the pediatrician's office, looking for an easy fix. The nurse failed to recognize a problem. I was on my own.

For nine months, my plan had been to take a three month leave of absence from my job as casualty claims adjuster for an insurance company. I thought I was being magnanimous. After all most maternity leave lasted a mere six weeks. No daycare center would be good enough for our precious girl when I returned to work. Instead, we opted for a caregiver who was an experienced mother, providing child care in her home.

Finding Ruby was a true blessing, but the strangest thing happened back in the office. My mind kept drifting from my work to my baby. I wasn't worried that Rachel wasn't well-cared for. I was wondering if I was missing out on something important. Helping people get their wrecked cars fixed and paying their medical expenses suddenly seemed pretty trivial when weighed against the value of my child's life. My perspective was beginning to shift.

By the time I picked her up and got home, I was feeling miserably confused. Since I had stayed home for three months, I knew the daily routine. It really wasn't much fun. If I kept working fulltime, I could already predict what the weekly schedule would be. There would be no time for fun.

Following my second day back at work, I was in my kitchen mechanically making preparations for dinner. As I tried to sort through my jumbled thoughts, a voice interrupted me. The voice said, **"When I called you to be a mother, I meant for that to be your job."**

I stopped in my tracks, holding an ice cube tray just removed from the freezer. I'm fairly sure the voice was not audible, but it was so clear, it could have been. My response came softly from my lips. "Ohhh," was all I could say as the blinders lifted, and I caught a glimpse of the enormity of my assignment.

This time I did not argue with God. This time I knew in a moment what I must do. The next day I gave my employer two weeks' notice. The following week my husband was offered a job transfer from Kansas City, Missouri, to Atlanta, Georgia. For him to accept the position would have required me to quit work anyway. The order and timing of events were simply confirmation that I was acting in the Lord's will, and I had a peaceful assurance that I could trust Him with our future.

2 Guardian Parents

While writing this book, I checked my memory for any parenting seminars or workshops I had attended. I could not recall a single one. My recollection included numerous seminars and retreats that emphasized spiritual growth, marriage enrichment, and home education, but none on the important subject of parenting.

We have all heard the cliché that kids are not born with instruction manuals included. Many of us just stumble along doing the best we know how to do. If we think our parents deserved a passing grade on how they raised us, we consciously, or unconsciously, model what they did. If we think our parents blew it more than getting it right, then we try to do everything differently.

I see two broad stroke approaches that a couple can take in how they view their parenting assignment. Out of those will flow the type of relationships we have with our children, and they will serve as the basis for many future decisions.

The first is **ownership.** A parent who sees himself as owner will think, "This is *my* child. God gave him to me, and I am responsible for establishing all the rules and boundaries. I am in charge of his upbringing and determining the course of his life for at least the next eighteen years. My reward will be a moral adult who is a productive citizen, loves God, and has the admiration of the world."

Sounds like a tall order. In fact, it sounds like a job for "super parent." Super parents are very vigilant. Heaven forbid that they should err. They are attempting to raise a little Mary Poppins—"practically perfect in every way." The pressure they apply to their children is only slightly less than the pressure they apply to themselves.

The second perspective is that of **guardianship.** A parent who sees himself as the guardian and *God* as the owner will think, "If I raise this child according to Biblical principles, seeking God for life direction, I can trust that the resulting adult will be one who brings glory to his Creator, and that will be my reward."

Still no small task, but the pressure is off the parent and on the Lord, who is strong and completely faithful.

God also has another key quality that mortals lack. He is omniscient. That means "all knowing in the present and in the future." Although we moms have given it a valiant effort through the centuries, we never have and never will achieve omniscience. Could it be that Mom doesn't always know best?

With God in the role of owner, then it is to Him and only Him that we are accountable. There are parents who believe themselves accountable to their own parents, their children's grandparents. If that is the case, then perhaps they don't see themselves as fully independent, capable adults. Honestly, did your parents always know best? Did they raise perfect children? As far as always pleasing them, you *know* from experience that sometimes no matter how hard you try, it just doesn't happen.

What has become more prevalent in today's topsy-turvy world is the belief that parents are accountable to their children. How did this happen?

I want to place partial blame on Sigmund Freud because of his influence on psychology and psychiatry. Trained therapists insistently told patients, "You are the way you are because of your father/mother." Not wanting to give our own kids the slightest excuse to place blame on us, we've decided to allow the kids to call the shots. If your goal is to please your children, I promise you will be even less successful at pleasing them than you were at pleasing your parents!

If we discard our goals of pleasing our parents, pleasing our children, or even pleasing ourselves, then wisdom says we need to strive to please the Lord.

Romans 14:17–18 tells us we gain God's approval by serving Christ and living in righteousness, peace, and joy in the Holy Spirit. Nowhere in God's word does it tell us to seek the approval of others. Certainly our hope is that by pleasing the Lord we will also attain human approval, particularly of those who love us. However, we must be mindful that the approval of man is secondary. As any politician will tell you, people's approval is fickle.

At the heart of the ownership-guardianship issue is *trust versus control*. Are we willing to put the reins that guide our children into God's hands, or will we grasp those reins tightly in our fists? If we insist on doing it our way, get ready for a wild ride!

Doesn't God know you better than you know yourself? He created your inmost being and knit you together in your mother's womb. (Ps. 139:13 NIV) That means He also knows your son or daughter even better than you do. He loves them with an everlasting love that cannot be diminished, and that's exactly the way He loves you, too. Yes, He knows you are at best an imperfect sinner, struggling to survive for an appointed time on planet earth while trying to prepare for an afterlife, which you hope will be vastly better. Yet the Lord entrusted YOU to care for other human lives when he made you a parent. What was He thinking?

I believe God was expecting the trust to be reciprocal. If He's going to trust you, then certainly you need to trust Him. He's made you a guardian of his highest creation. As a guardian, your role is to guard and protect your children's bodies, minds, and spirits.

Protecting Bodies

Mothers have an almost instinctive desire to protect their young, and this kicks in with the realization that they are carrying a life. Many female smokers and alcohol imbibers suddenly have the will to quit because the effects of tobacco and alcohol on the unborn have been well-documented.

Following the baby's birth, every prepared parent brings their infant home in a properly installed car seat. No doubt about it. Physical protection is priority one because your precious offspring is fragile and defenseless.

That is why it is so shockingly disturbing when we hear a parent has defied his or her natural instinct and has caused grave harm to his own flesh and blood. It's so out of order that we can't wrap our minds around it.

Let's be honest. Perhaps some of us have had a fleeting thought of doing something to our child that we *know* is completely wrong. That is NOT an indicator that you are an awful parent. If you are feeling self-condemnation, please remind yourself that the Lord's forgiveness is readily available. "If we confess our sins to Him, He is faithful to forgive us our sins and to cleanse us from all wickedness." (I John 1:9 NLT)

Just as importantly, you must forgive yourself. Acknowledge that you did *not* act upon that thought, and next thank God for His restraint.

I have heard interviews with women who were diagnosed and truly suffered with post partum depression. Many of us have experienced some days of "baby blues" in those early months. Magnifying those feelings one hundred times may give us a glimpse of their despair.

As stated earlier, I was definitely a nervous new mom. Before Rachel was born I had a dream. In my dream I had a baby, but somehow that fact was temporarily gone from my awareness. Of course later I realized that it's impossible to just "forget" about an infant, but in the dream I left her unattended in her crib for a day or even two. When at last I remembered to go into her room, she was alive, but weak. Oh, but how that dream scared me!

In the days following her birth, my nerves were so over-active that I got hives for the first and only time in my life. Since hives itch, naturally I scratched. The scratching caused large patches of skin to become raised and red. My doctor prescribed an ointment with the admonition to stop scratching.

Typically the itching got worse at night. When I became more cognizant of the onset of itching, I also became aware of what I was doing just prior to the onset. I was worrying about my baby. As I tried to go to sleep, I was wondering how many hours before she woke up. Would I hear her cries immediately? Had she gotten enough to eat that day? Was it too warm or too cool in her room? My thoughts literally caused nerve endings in my body to be overly sensitized.

I will never forget the night when I thought I had reached the end of my rope. It followed a day of doing little except trying to meet my newborn's needs, and apparently I was doing a poor job. Here it was nearly midnight, she was *still* crying, and I just couldn't take it. Frustration with her and with myself was mounting. I carried her to my room, stood at my husband's bedside in the dark, and allowed the crying to awaken him. I held her horizontally above him, and calmly said, "If you don't take this baby, I'm going to bounce her off the walls."

With no hesitation and no questions, he arose and took Rachel from my arms. He retreated to her room and within ten minutes, she was sleeping.

My maternal incompetence was again confirmed, but now there was the added weight of guilt that I'd had this horrible thought and had spoken that thought aloud. Not for a second do I believe I would have acted on it. I think they were words spoken from exhaustion and desperation for relief, and likely I wanted to dramatize the point, but still I must be a horrible person to say such a horrible thing.

Certainly that's what Satan would have us believe. What the word of God says is that the Lord's mercies are new every morning, and it is because of His great love that we are not consumed. (Lamentations 3:22-23) Self-condemnation can eat us alive if we focus on our failings; yet every day our Father gives us another chance, and the next day He gives us still another chance. We don't have to repeat yesterday's mistakes. Yes, there may be consequences for yesterday's choices, but the slate for today is clean.

Protecting health

One of the most significant means of protection of our children's health is prayer. If I'm stating the obvious, then why aren't more parents using Christ's authority over sickness as often as they run to the pediatrician's office?

When you know there's a virus going around, do you mentally accept the fact that most likely your kids will get it because that's what usually happens? Or do you plead the blood of Jesus over everyone in the household and declare boldly that no virus will enter in?

One fall the flu prognostications alarmed me, and I began considering whether or not we should all get vaccinated. In prayer the Holy Spirit showed me that I was not to fear, and the action I needed to take involved no needles. I was to declare that my house was the Lord's property, and that no viruses had the right of entry. Of course, our bodies are His, too, and our bodies were also off limits.

I asked God to put a shield at every doorway, so that if a guest should be carrying a "bug", it would drop dead when it hit that shield. If anyone in our family unwittingly picked up any kind of sickness-causing germ, I asked God to destroy those bacteria before they came into the house.

Wielding this battle in the spirit took only minutes, but the effects lasted for months. Not only did all five of us avoid vomiting, diarrhea, fevers, etc, but none of us caught even the slightest of colds. Naturally, this experience increased my gratitude to our loving, protective Father, and also greatly increased my faith.

A few years later our family was in the position of having a sharply reduced income and no health insurance for nearly a year. My testimony is that reliance on the Lord is far better than reliance on the most solid insurance company.

During this time of no medical insurance, I regularly prayed for protection from injuries as well as taking a stand against viruses. As all parents know, accidents can happen to any kid at any time. Even minor ones can send us rushing to get stitches or x-rays, and the ER is not cheap.

Once again God demonstrated his loving care. Our guardian angels' performance went above and beyond. Upon later reflection, I marveled that we had not chalked up *even one* doctor's office visit. For a family of five to not need a doctor's care for more than a year is getting close to the miraculous.

Please be clear that I'm not advocating that you put God to the test and cancel your health insurance benefits. I'm simply saying that when you find yourself in situations that are beyond your ability to control, remember that God is not surprised, and He is delighted to step in and show Himself strong on your behalf.

There is nothing that is outside the Lord's circle of care surrounding our bodies. Our son was age four when warts started appearing on his fingers. The medical books say warts are caused by a virus, but the source of the virus was baffling. No one else in the family or any of his playmates had warts. They were not at all painful, he didn't seem bothered by them in the least, but I thought they were unattractive.

I bought some over-the-counter wart remover, followed the directions, but saw no effect. In fact, over the months the original ones seemed to be growing a bit larger, and they were multiplying. Other treatments for warts include having them burned off or cut off in a doctor's office, but I didn't want to put him through that when I knew there was no guarantee that the warts would not grow back.

One afternoon I was in a doctor's waiting room, flipping through a magazine, when I spied a short article in which readers had contributed their home remedy cures that have worked for them. You guessed it. This particular issue included advice from several people on how to get rid of warts.

One novel suggestion especially caught my attention. It said to rub a raw potato on the warts a couple times and they would disappear. Seriously? There was no explanation of why this would work, but the writer swore that it would.

At times I wonder if the word "gullible" is written on my forehead, but hey, this "surefire" cure was simple, so why not try it? At home that night I cut a potato in half and rubbed the inside of it all over my little boy's fingers, and at the same time I prayed aloud that God would completely remove the warts. I wish I could say that my prayer was drenched in faith, but actually my faith was no bigger than the small wart.

I repeated the process two or three more times in the next days, and then my mind moved on to other things. Probably two weeks passed before I carefully examined my son's hands. Not only were all seven warts GONE, I couldn't even see a trace of where they'd been! How awesome was that!

It left me wondering "Was it the potato, or was it the prayer, or was it a combination of both?" I've never known the answer, but either way it was definitely God's loving provision and a permanent solution because my son has never had another wart.

Protecting minds

It's difficult to separate protection of minds from protection of spirits, but here I'm going to limit my reference to the mind only, because spiritual warfare warrants its own discussion in a separate chapter.

To my way of thinking, protecting a child's mind deals with

knowledge—what he should know and the manner in which he comes to know it.

One error specifically that has become more common in the "information age" is giving a child more information than is needed, or providing children information that is not age-appropriate. For many in today's world, there are no longer taboo subjects. Americans seem to think it's perfectly okay to talk about anything with just about anybody. Openness and honesty are openly embraced, but discretion has been elbowed out.

It's likely Eve may have been the first mother whose offspring asked the question that makes mommies squirm. "Where do babies come from?"

It's a safe guess that her reply was, "From God". What else would she have said? I can't imagine that she launched into some detailed explanation or pulled out the lifecycle encyclopedia complete with color diagrams. Perhaps Eve herself had a few questions as to the origins of Cain and Abel! After all, she and Adam had arrived on earth without an egg and sperm uniting, without benefit of a uterus. Eve had no mom to fill in the blanks and teach her the facts of life.

My point is that under age ten, most children are quite satisfied with general answers to life's big questions. A halfway astute parent can gauge from their questions how much they may already know. Don't be evasive, and don't say you'll tell them everything when they're older. That's a surefire way to arouse even greater curiosity. Just keep your answer short. Keeping it simple and brief works well for *any* topic that is beyond a child's ability to fully comprehend.

The area of finances can also be a pitfall where parents sometimes give too much information. Little shoulders of children should not have to bear the burdens of the parents!

A family's limited finances can be a teaching tool if handled wisely. For example, if Dad loses his job, it's good to explain that the family will first spend money on the essentials. Then go over your priority list so they will understand what you consider essential. You can bet the kids aren't thinking of the electric bill or car insurance!

Ask them to think of ways the family can spend less. Their answers may surprise you. Try to reach some agreements so that when you pass McDonald's for the umpteenth time without stopping and the whining begins, you can remind them of the family's decision. Some of their suggestions might be amusing (skipping vegetables), but some will be practical and unselfish. If children feel a sense of teamwork, the financial storm will be better weathered.

The undesirable way to handle a situation where Dad loses his job would be to have them see you go into panic mode. They do not need to hear comments like, "I just don't know what we're going to do", or "we might have to sell one of the cars", or "we could lose the house".

Be careful to not even let them *overhear* such statements. Instead let your words and your prayers demonstrate faith and dependence on the Lord to provide for every need.

One of the hardest things we ever had to tell our three children was that they would not be returning to their Christian school the following year. For nine years we'd been so grateful for Christian education, and three years earlier we'd been a founding family when a new school was launched.

However, we needed to relieve the financial strain we'd been under, and the next year's hefty tuition increase left no doubt what must be done. Seeing their tears was heart-wrenching, and I cried with them. At the time God hadn't given us a clear new direction to share, but that next school year was filled with surprises and blessings we could not have anticipated.

My observation has been that it is easy, especially for single mothers, to forget that their children are not little adults. Without another adult to discuss pressing concerns or even the events of the day, it's so easy to talk to the person in closest proximity. Often that's the eldest child. Not only is it unfair to expect your child to give you emotional support, it's also selfish.

In a marriage, reciprocity is a reasonable expectation, but parenting a child is not intended to be a reciprocal relationship. There's nothing balanced about it. The scales are heavily weighted on the parental side.

The child takes and the adult gives. The child keeps taking, and the adult keeps giving. Ideally, when the child reaches adult maturity in his twenties, then it becomes a more balanced relationship.

What happens if the single mother doesn't attempt to have her emotional needs legitimately met through another adult (friend, pastor, counselor, her own parent), but sucks her child in? The emotional growth of the child slows down. Often these kids *appear* to be more mature because some of their childhood innocence and lightheartedness was exchanged for sobering reality and a sense of duty. It was not a fair trade.

Instead of being better prepared and equipped to operate independently, as young adults they may shrink from launching out on their own. Unlike physical weights that build strength and endurance, the weight of emotional baggage on a child over time makes him weaker, not stronger.

The baggage and far-reaching effects upon children raised in an alcoholic home environment have been chronicled by the volumes. Many were forced into caretaker roles at far too young an age. Life was serious business and there was little time for play and frivolity.

According to Dr. Janet Geringer Woititz, author of the best-seller *Adult Children of Alcoholics,* these children grow up into adults who take themselves very seriously and who find it difficult to just have fun. Many are super responsible, and in their attempt to control their world, they try to manage everything and everyone. As we know, that's a path leading to frustration and isolation.

Another area where it has become increasingly important to protect our children's minds is the news media. If you listen to news from a metropolitan outlet, there isn't a day where terrible events are not reported. Reporters and camera operators seem to believe their job is to provide us with all the gruesome details.

Parents, please be aware of your child's exposure to the news. The catastrophe on 9/11/01 brought a sharp awareness of media's impact to thousands of households for the first time. It's sad that it took something of such magnitude for people to wake up. Many parents made the conscientious decision to not allow those images to be transferred from their TV screens to the mental screens of their young children. They were correct in doing so.

In a child's world, one doesn't have to search far to find tangible things that frighten. Even a large, friendly dog can be as frightening as a T-rex. To bring scary things into the home via media and allow children exposure to them shows a lack of sound judgment and discernment.

This calls to mind the topics of movies and video games. Any discussion of these would be like poking the proverbial hornets' nest, and these subjects have been thoroughly hashed.

I'm going to keep it simple and make two statements. First, the movie rating guide of General, Parental Guidance, PG 13, etc. has very limited value and should be approached with skepticism. Second, unless you've checked with a source that critiques from a Christian worldview, or gotten a personal recommendation from a trusted party, I would not allow my children to view a movie that I had not first watched myself. You may say that's inconvenient. I say that's a small price to pay for protection of an innocent, impressionable mind.

To list every safeguard of protection for children's bodies and minds is not possible. A few examples to prompt your thinking and your prayers have been given. What you choose to do, or not do, is up to you. The Holy Spirit will be your guide in all things if you yield to His direction.

3 A Trial Amid Blessings

In the year following Rachel's birth I had read a couple articles stating there might be a relationship between the use of birth control pills and miscarriages. Specifically, it was thought, but not proven, that taking oral contraceptives between pregnancies increased the chances of miscarriage. So knowing how easily I'd gotten pregnant the first time, I chose to err on the side of caution and opt for other types of birth control.

When I thought the timing was right, I conceived and my second pregnancy was even better. This time I was not having morning sickness and my weight gain was slower, so by the time of my second pre-natal visit, I had gained just three pounds and felt terrific. It was week fifteen when Dr. Ratchford put his stethoscope to my belly to listen to the baby's heartbeat. He was unable to detect it, but insisted there was no cause for alarm because "It's still early."

Three days later I began spotting, called the doctor's office, and was assured that some spotting was not out of the ordinary. The usual explanation is that when the embryo burrows deeper into the walls of the uterus, blood vessels are often broken. Two more days passed. It was Saturday evening, and the bleeding was heavier. Also I was feeling some mild cramps after being on my feet for several hours while on a tour of homes.

Concerned but not panicked, I called my doctor on Sunday. He calmly asked me to come in on Monday morning. A rapid pregnancy test revealed that indeed I was still pregnant, and a pelvic exam told him that my cervix was soft and expanding the way it should. However, Dr. Ratchford believed a sonogram was in order, and since his office was not equipped for that, he wanted me to check in next door at Piedmont Hospital.

Jack came to the rescue, arranging for the sitter to keep Rachel until mid-afternoon and packing an overnight bag for me. Meanwhile, my bleeding had subsided and I underwent my first ultrasound.

One of Ratchford's associates, Dr. Moreland, came to my room later to report what the sonographer had told him. He asked me how far along I was, and I told him this was the beginning of the sixteenth week.

He countered with, "Are you sure?" "What was the date of your last period?" At that point he left the room to call the technician because he had not seen the ultrasound images himself.

When he returned, I learned the reason for his confusion. The sonogram indicated a pregnancy of no more than six weeks— not sixteen. For reasons unknown, the baby had stopped developing. Telling me that Dr. Ratchford would discuss what should be done, Dr. Moreland expressed his sympathy and left me alone to digest the devastating news.

I was absolutely in shock, but needed to release the emotion building inside me. How I dealt with it was to enter the bathroom, close the door, put my hand over my mouth, and let out a controlled scream. It was controlled because the last thing I wanted was a nurse rushing in. With Jack at home on childcare duty, it was a long, lonely night.

During morning rounds Dr. Ratchford explained that my body should have spontaneously miscarried many weeks earlier. In situations where a miscarriage fails to occur naturally, it is referred to as a "missed abortion."

There were two options. I could have a dilation and curettage procedure done that day, or I could go home and wait for the inevitable miscarriage. Then an emergency D and C would be required. My choice was to just get done with it, so when I left the hospital that afternoon, I was no longer pregnant, but physically I felt no different than I had two days before.

Because I felt fine, my mind had difficulty coming to terms with what had happened. Combined with a sense of unreality was a sense of terrible loss. I had anticipated a child who held all the promise and potential of a Rachel, and suddenly that child was gone.

My body had played a cruel trick on me. There I was, thinking everything was going great while everything was very wrong. For the first time, my female parts did not function the way they were supposed to. My body had betrayed and deceived me. Why, God? If I had to lose the baby, surely the disappointment would have been easier to bear earlier, rather than later.

Everywhere I went I encountered pregnant women. They were shopping at the mall, attending church, buying groceries, filling up at gas stations. How dare they! A glance at their rounded bellies sent a stab of intense envy into my flat gut.

After three weeks of misery and self-pity, I heard my pastor preach on the subject of praising God when circumstances are unfavorable and undesirable. The Holy Spirit was nailing me. I knew I held the key to my own happiness. If I had any hope of getting peace, I had to choose to speak words of praise and thankfulness with my lips. It didn't matter that I was saying them through gritted teeth. It didn't matter if my tone was a bit angry.

Praising caused my heart to begin to get into alignment with the words from my mouth, and that made it possible for emotional healing to begin. Praising God when things are tough, when it's the last thing you feel like doing, is one of the most important spiritual truths I've ever learned. When Jesus said, "In this world you *will* have trouble, you *will* have problems," He wasn't kidding.

"I will praise you forever for what you have done; in your name I will hope, for your name is good. I will praise you in the presence of your saints." (Psalm 52: 9 NIV)

"Give thanks to the Lord, for he is good; his love endures forever." (Psalm 118: 1 NIV)

A Sister is a Precious Gift

My doctor advised waiting three months before trying to get pregnant. That was a reasonable request. What seemed unreasonable was that I failed to conceive in the fourth month—and the fifth month. What irony that my period started on the due date of the baby I lost.

At that point I started making wild guesses as to what might be happening. Did I have some undetected physical condition? Was God trying to teach me something else?

What if I never had another baby? Not acceptable. You see, I intended to keep a vow I had made in my youth. I grew up with several "onlies". That's a name for kids who don't have brothers or sisters. To not have a sibling seemed to me a terrible thing, and I had vowed that I would NEVER bring up just one child because it would be so unfair. Surely God would not have me defy my long-entrenched beliefs in this area. Or would He?

All doubts were set aside when I did conceive, and this pregnancy seemed to mimic the morning sickness and weight gain I had experienced the first time. These were positive signs for which I could truly rejoice and be thankful.

Because I had not experienced the blessing of growing up with a sister (whom I very much hoped for when my third brother was born), my current desire was that I could present Rachel with a baby sister. Two girls would be twice the fun, and the pink outfits would be worn again.

As my doctor practiced medicine conservatively and saw no need for an ultrasound this time, I didn't get a picture that might have provided confirmation of the baby's sex. That was okay because I concluded that since the Lord had given me the name "Julia" (another Biblical name) I must be having a girl.

Only two weeks from the due date, a slight complication took me by surprise. Dr. Ratchford discovered that the baby was sitting upright, rather than doing a normal headstand. In medical terminology the baby was a "frank breech". Already too big for the doctor to maneuver into the correct position, he assured me there was little cause for concern.

First, because I had already successfully delivered a baby, I had what he called a "proven pelvis". Equally important was that Dr. Ratchford had done his internship at Grady Memorial Hospital in downtown Atlanta, and there he'd gained lots of experience delivering breech babies. He was confident in letting nature take its course, but if I wanted to opt for a C-section, he would comply with my wishes.

Believe me, it was very tempting to pick my own delivery date and make plans accordingly. Rachel arrived twelve days past her due date, and that waiting game was not fun! Fortunately, accounts of longer post-partum recovery times with Caesarians gave me a reality check, so I chose to go into labor naturally and attempt a vaginal delivery.

The Lord was so good to me! Not only did I deliver a strong, healthy baby girl without a C-section, but even with the extra time needed to push her down the birth canal, the labor was still shorter and easier. An added plus was the fact that she was born one day before the due date. Hallelujah!

Although Jack and I missed our clue at the time, in retrospect we saw that Julia's breech birth was a flashing warning sign as to what we could expect from our cuddly package. Clearly she was her own little person, determinedly going through life on her own terms.

There was another significant pre-natal clue which I had ignored. During the last trimester I barely felt any movement from her during the course of my day. In the evening when I'd completed the chores and was ready for "down" time, those little arms and legs would begin thrusting vigorously for several hours until I dropped off to sleep.

While I had heard about babies getting their days and nights mixed up, sleeping more during the day than at night, Jack and I were completely unprepared for what lay ahead. Following the pattern she established in the womb, Julia basically just slept and ate during the day, usually awake for intervals of only sixty to ninety minutes. However, about eight o'clock every evening, her eyes would pop wide open, and thus began several hours of alert wakefulness. When babies want to sleep, it's nearly impossible to keep them awake; when they are not tired, it's really impossible to get them to sleep.

My husband and I started sleeping in shifts. After nursing her, I'd go to bed at ten. Then Jack would wake me around midnight, ready for his turn to sleep. Because he had to go to work the next day, she was my responsibility until whatever time I could get her to settle down, which on average was two a.m. Thank the Lord her wakefulness was not accompanied by fussiness! Sure, she demanded a reasonable amount of attention, but at least she wasn't screaming at the top of her lungs.

Sleep-deprived and desperate, we tried walking with her in a Snugli, walking without a Snugli, pushing her around the house in the stroller, and of course, the time-tested infant swing. Our baby swing paid for itself many times over, but those automatic, nonstop ones were not yet on the market. Julia loved the back and forth movement, and when her "toy" stopped, those feet started kicking and the whimpering beckoned her servant parent to crank the swing into high gear again.

Gradually we attained the goal of getting our baby to sleep from midnight to six. It was real progress. Then came a huge setback that sent me tailspinning toward depression and simultaneously feeling ridiculous. What happened? Daylight Savings Time happened.

A trivial event in the lives of millions of Americans, but for me it was akin to a disaster. Weeks of effort were undone by the simple act of setting clocks ahead one hour. As that dreaded day approached, and I was helpless to stop it, I told myself that I was *not* going to be the first person to ever cry over a time change!

With God's help, all three of us adjusted and survived. Infant Rachel had started sleeping through the night by age three weeks. (Of course, the tradeoff was her daytime catnaps.) While Julia's bedtime had become respectable by eight months, it was still troubling to me that she woke up once or twice every night.

On a day when I was more tired and frustrated than usual, I vented to the Lord. "Why, Lord? I've been asking You for months to change Julia's sleep schedule. Others have been praying, too. (Mentally their faces flashed before me.) Yet You haven't truly answered our prayers and changed her."

I paused and God answered. He said, "*You're* the one that needs to change."

"Me?" ME? Why do I need to change?"

"You need to love and accept her just the way she is."

Oh, my! Yes, I loved my sweet baby girl. I'd throw myself in front of a truck to save her, but a part of me had not been willing to accept her *just the way she was.* I had been focused on trying to alter her internal clock so she would become a baby on a good schedule.

God's words were a serious wakeup call and taught me an important lesson. He actually wants us to treat our children the same way He treats His—with love and acceptance, just the way we are. Imagine that. From that point I stopped fretting and embraced Julia in my heart more fully—just the way she was.

Blessing Number Three

While I was in the hospital, in labor with Julia, Jack made some comment about "the next time." No doubt he was attempting to add levity to the moment, but husbands take note. During labor is not the best time to introduce the possibility of a future pregnancy!

The whole experience of Julia's birth had been so grace-filled that I felt like a true overcomer. It was one of those times when I could say, "I can do all things through Christ," with the weight of total belief.

At some point I told the Lord that if He wanted me to have a third child, I would be okay with that. If it wasn't His plan, that would be fine, too. My feelings were in the neutral range, just slightly more pro than con. The last thing I wanted to do was forge ahead and have another baby if that wasn't God's best for our whole family. BUT (here it comes) if a third child was to be, I wanted children numbers two and three to be born closer together than children one and two. That was my sole condition. The difference in the girls' ages was three years, eight months, putting them four years apart in school. My ideal spacing would be three years.

Additionally, I had heard a woman's testimony in regard to praying about a life-changing decision. Her prayer was for God to either increase or decrease her desire, according to what He wanted her to do. Over time her desire had increased, and this was pivotal as she reached a point of decision.

This approach sounded good to me, and since it had worked for her, why not? I prayed, "Lord, if you want me to have another child, let my desire increase, and if you do *not* want me to have another child, cause my desire to decrease."

Two or three months later, I did a self-check. It seemed to me that I was now less interested in having another baby. Thoughts of babies had become less frequent. So I proceeded in this manner: regularly examining my heart while not regularly using birth control, but not "trying" either.

On the career front, Jack was making plans to leave the headhunting agency where he'd worked for ten years and to start his own business. He'd made a name for himself in the industry, with an impressive list of client companies. Initially, he would be the sole recruiter, but during the next school year, I was going to work in the office on Mondays and Tuesdays to help with ad response, scheduling, etc. I was looking forward to assisting him and to working beyond the walls of my house.

Just weeks after the business venture began, I discovered I was pregnant. I wish I could say that I was thrilled and joyful, but actually I was shocked and depressed. Why hadn't my "increase or decrease my desire for a baby" prayer worked? Why had God waited until I started making plans in a different direction to set me on His course? I had truly believed I was being guided as I sought His will. Instead of dealing with me gently, I felt like my Lord had taken me by the shoulders and turned me 180 degrees in a different direction. Now instead of having children closer together, they would be nearly five years apart.

Compounding my woe was the fact that my due date was January 4. To truly grasp how devastating this was, you had to have been born right after the biggest holiday week of the entire year. My birthday is January 2, and I'd always hated having it completely overshadowed by the celebrations of Christmas and New Year's. Grandmothers and aunts disregarded a girl's feelings every time they gave me a Christmas present and said, "This is for your birthday, too." Now I would be presenting my own child with a lousy birth date no better than my own.

For a month I struggled to get to a place of peaceful acceptance in regard to my pregnancy. Where I wanted to be— where I knew I should be— was in a place of joyful anticipation.

God used a sermon by my pastor, Dr. Paul L. Walker, to speak powerfully to me at this time. The title was "Reversing the Reverses" and was based on the life of Joseph in Genesis. The primary points were: God is working in my life. He has placed me in a strategic position. He will bring about an outcome that is for good.

Sounds plainly obvious and simple, but when you question whether God even remembers your address, a straightforward message of hope can create a big impact. As I privately pondered the teaching, the Lord spoke directly to me, telling me I was bringing His special child into the world. That message of hope caused my faith to kick in, and my outlook became positive and happy. Belatedly, I could now begin to rejoice with others who were already rejoicing in my gift of new life.

Although I hadn't even had my first prenatal visit, in my spirit I was convinced I was carrying a boy, and I knew what his middle name had to be—Joseph—a man who reversed the reverses in his life. Joseph was also my dad's name, and it was the opinion of a biased daughter that I could name my son after no finer man walking the face of earth.

4 The Spiritual Battle for the Life of Your Child

Keeping in my mind the concept of parents as guardians, there is one remaining part of a child—his spirit—that requires careful attention. Of body, mind, and spirit, it is the spirit that is most frequently neglected.

In this chapter I want to speak in specifics regarding the battle that is being waged for the life of your child. Our examination needs to go beyond the usual broad, generalized terms in which people speak of the battle between good and evil. Dear brothers and sisters, God does not want us to be ignorant about these battles for our children. If you are lifting your brow right now and wondering "What is she talking about? Who is fighting?", then prepare to have your spiritual eyes opened. Let's pray.

Father, I come to You asking that by Your grace You impart to us a clear revelation of Your truth. I ask for your direction in showing us how to apply it within our homes. I acknowledge that each person in Your creation is uniquely made, and You have a purpose for each to fulfill. Teach us how to set a spiritual climate for our homes that facilitates Your perfect will being done in our lives and in our families. Amen.

All of us were born into a sinful world with sinful natures. Most everyone readily agrees with the sinful world part, but some are thinking, "Aren't most people basically good?"

Quite the opposite is true. Our legacy from Adam and Eve is to be born with a natural propensity to do the opposite of what God has told us to do. If this were not so, then God would not have found it necessary to sacrifice his own perfect son to atone for our sins.

Consider what is natural for a baby. Babies are the epitome of selfishness. Their primary concern is getting their needs met. When they are hungry, babies don't care if mom is hungry, too, or that dad needs his sleep so that he can go to work in a few hours. Their whole orientation is "me, me, me". That's why God had to make them so cute and adorable that parents willingly place infants' immediate needs above their own!

Seriously though, the baby who never learns that he/she is not the center of the universe will grow into a tantrum-throwing toddler. That toddler will become an attention-demanding child, who grows into a spoiled brat. This is the natural progression, and that is why parental intervention is required every step of the way.

The answer to the question "Who is fighting?" has just one answer. God and the angels of light are battling Satan and his demons of darkness. As individuals we are on one side or the other. There is no neutral ground.

As saints we are provided with protective armor. Ephesians 6:11–13 (NLT) tells us, "Put on all of God's armor so that you will be able to stand firm against all strategies of the devil. For we are not fighting against flesh-and-blood enemies, but against evil rulers and authorities of the unseen world, against mighty powers in this dark world, and against evil spirits in the heavenly places."

Now that we know *who* is waging war, we must ask, "*Why* are they fighting?". Both God and Satan are actively recruiting for citizens of their respective kingdoms, commonly called heaven and hell. Now some may think that the battle doesn't really begin until a child reaches an age where he can understand what's right and what's wrong, or when he is able to reason. That is an idealistic but false notion, and in a moment I'll explain why.

"What determines the outcome of the battle?" Ultimately, it is individual choice or free will. Has the individual chosen to believe and live his life according to what God has declared to be true, or has the individual chosen to believe and live his life according to what Satan has declared to be true?

If only we could choose one time and be done with it. How easy that would be! Like it or not, we are required to keep on choosing throughout our lifetime. Our actions and lifestyle flow from our decisions. When our lives contradict our words, the devil smiles. Hypocrites are his friends.

My initial knowledge regarding demon spirits came straight from accounts given in the New Testament. In some instances, the spirits caused the possessed person to have seizures, be suicidal, or have supernatural strength. There were others who suffered blindness or the inability to speak. In every case, it was obvious that these individuals had lost control of themselves. In every case, however, the spirits had to submit to the authority of Jesus Christ or his disciples when they were commanded to depart from the person they inhabited.

This sums up what I knew about spirits affecting the lives of real people. I doubt I'd given much consideration to how they might be working in today's world, or even if they still were. Although I hadn't gone to see The Exorcist, I'd heard enough about it to know that none of that stuff could possibly occur. Through a situation with my daughter, the Lord was about to expand my knowledge and alter my perspective.

Julia had gone through the "terrible two's", which had not been so terrible. Then a few weeks following her third birthday, I saw a big change in her personality. To this day I have no idea if the change was precipitated by a particular event. It seemed to happen overnight.

It was as if she woke up one morning in a bad mood, and nothing could shake her out of it. My happy, contented little girl became just the opposite. She mostly fussed and whined, sometimes just lying on the floor, not responding to my attempts to comfort her with words or touch.

After several days, thinking she must be ill, we visited the pediatrician to see if there was an ear infection or anything else that would account for her behavior. The doctor found absolutely nothing wrong.

Now assured that there was no physical reason for the crankiness, I tended to deal with her more firmly than before, but to little effect. Each day was as miserable as the day before. I had shared with Jack some of my frustrations. One Saturday he stayed home with her for several hours and when I returned, the usually unruffled dad was frustrated himself. He told me nothing he offered had pleased her. She didn't want the lunch, didn't want the drink, didn't want to play, etc.

"This is what I've been telling you!"

"You mean she's like this every day?" Finally, he was getting it!

"Yes. I can't seem to please her either. If I give her orange juice, she wants apple juice. When I give her apple juice, then she cries because she didn't want it in the yellow cup. She wanted it in the green cup."

Then Jack said something that rattled me to the core. "There is something seriously wrong with her, and I think you need to find a child psychologist who can figure out what it is." He was very sincere.

Having my husband think something was seriously wrong with our daughter was equally as troubling to me as Julia's behavior. Just locating a child psychologist that was also a Christian, whose credentials were excellent, and someone I deemed trustworthy, seemed problematic in itself. I didn't know where to start, and my prayers for the whole situation became more earnest.

There was a thought that ran through my mind several times, and I honestly don't recall if I gave voice to it. The change in Julia was so radical that I kept thinking, "It's as if somebody came during the night, took my little angel, and left another child in her bed that looks just like her."

During this time I was part of a team of women who met weekly to prepare for a spiritual retreat. One night we divided into small groups for prayer. My group leader, Nancy, shared an insight she had gleaned from a Jack Hayford message. It revolved around how to deal with difficult situations. Pastor Hayford had said that shouting "grace" at even a mountain would cause it to break into pieces. "What are you, O great mountain? Before Zerubbabel you shall become a plain; and he shall bring forward the top stone amid shouts of 'Grace, grace to it!'" Zech. 4:7 (KJV)

Nancy felt she could apply "speaking grace" to problems she was having with her teenage son. As she spoke, the Holy Spirit confirmed that this word was also for me. I needed to speak grace to my daughter. Although I had no specific expectations, I was more than willing to give it a try. There was nothing to lose.

The next morning Julia got out of her bed and came into my room. I greeted her with "good morning", "how's my girl?", "what shall we have for breakfast?"

Without a word of response or facial reaction, she simply lay down on the floor with her blankey. She wanted to be near me, yet she was still withdrawn. It was sadly typical of how her days began of late. Kneeling on the floor, I scooped her into my arms.

"I love you, Julia, and Jesus loves you, too. In the name of Jesus, I am speaking grace into your spirit right now. Grace be unto you, Julia. Receive it in the name of Jesus. Grace. Grace."

I may have said more; I may have repeated. I know I continued to hold her until she squirmed to be released. I had spoken very quietly, and she had remained silent.

As I proceeded to the kitchen to prepare breakfast, she followed me only as far as the family room. I could hear sounds that she was getting out toys, so it was several minutes before I went back to check on her. She was engaged in play, but when she noticed me, she got up and started chatting as she walked toward me. She looked happy! She sounded happy! In truth, she was happier than she had been in three weeks!

The difference in her was amazing, and I was astounded! Lord, it really worked! Thank you!

For the next two hours, Julia was herself again. Then for no apparent reason, the crankiness returned. It was time for the second dose of spiritual medicine.

Again I hugged her as I whispered, "Grace be unto you, Julia, in the name of Jesus. Grace and peace. I want you to receive this into your spirit right now."

Once again the same incredible results occurred within just a few minutes. This was beyond wonderful! If all it took was a few well-chosen words to bring out a sunny disposition, I could keep this up indefinitely!

When she awoke from her afternoon nap, she seemed eager to rejoin the world, but within an hour, she was becoming grumpy. I had not detected a trigger. It was like an internal switch got flipped, and she went from "on" to "off", but I didn't know what was flipping the switch.

Now when I discover something that works, for sure I intend to stick with it, so I did not hesitate to draw her close to me and to begin saying the words of grace. Now she stiffened in my arms and resisted being held, so I hugged her tighter. When she spoke, the lower pitch of her voice caught me by surprise.

"I don't like it when you say that grace stuff."

My eyes widened and my jaw probably dropped as I pulled back and looked straight into Julia's face. I *knew* that it was not my daughter who had spoken. Yes, the words had come from her mouth, but they hadn't come from *her*.

Firmly and calmly I told her, "I know you don't like it, but I'm going to keep on saying it. You *are* going to hear it. Grace and peace be to you in the name of Jesus! Receive His grace and peace and love right now into your spirit!"

I released her. There was no further argument, and Julia resumed her play as if nothing had happened. Isn't it cool how children can do that? I'd just had a life-changing revelation that I didn't fully understand and couldn't explain. I needed to call a time-out so I could sort through it, but the world just went on.

The next day I spoke grace to Julia on two occasions, and the day after that, just once. The switch stayed "on" for days, then weeks at a time, but if it flipped, I knew it. God had shown me how to recognize the difference between legitimate discontentment with a natural cause, and discontentment that originated from spiritual distress.

Creating Havoc

It is my belief that evil spirits desire to torment. Webster defines this verb "to afflict with great, usually incessant or repeated bodily or mental suffering," "to throw into commotion; stir up, disturb."

The book of Revelation leaves no doubt that hell is a real place of torture and torment. Hell has been home to Satan and his legions since before recorded time, so that's eons' worth of torment they've endured. Could it be that demons take their behavior cues from their environment in the same way that people do? Some ministers deny the existence of demon spirits, but those who do recognize that they still operate on the earth seem to agree that their mission is to inflict torment in some fashion or degree. Escalated torment becomes torture which is defined as "extreme anguish of body or mind; agony".

Remember the demon-possessed man who confronted Jesus? (Luke 8:27–30) No shackles and chains could bind him. He was naked and had been living in a cemetery. The first thing Jesus did was to command the evil spirit to come out, but the spirit screams, "Please don't torture me."

What a bold request. The spirit that had been inflicting torture pleads to not be tortured. Further questioning by Jesus reveals the man has not one, but a legion of evil spirits all bent on the victim's ultimate destruction. Up against power that exceeded their own, they begged Jesus to not send them into the abyss or the underworld. Even pagan religions believed the underworld to be a place of torture.

In civilized societies today, we don't come across too many people residing naked in cemeteries. If we did, I don't think "possessed" is what would pop into folks' minds. More likely the term used would be "mentally ill".

"Mentally ill" we can accept and at least partially understand. We've come up with all sorts of ways to treat those who have been diagnosed as mentally ill. We put them in hospitals, give them medication, put them in therapy, etc. These treatments have varying measures of success, but doctors never pronounce mentally ill individuals to be "cured." The goal of a medical practitioner is to manage the mental illness as best as is possible.

Here's the big *What If.* What if spirits still torment and torture folks today?

I believe they do. I believe that attacks by spirits can originate and occur in a variety of ways. I also think that attacks can be external to the body as well as internal. They may be generalized rather than focused on an individual. Let me share some events that occurred in our household.

We accepted a transfer to Atlanta, Georgia, while Rachel was still an infant. I was blessed to have movers do most of the packing, but the downside was that I was in the house more than a week before I found the box containing the silverware. As the months passed and various items were temporarily lost or misplaced, I didn't think it unusual. After all, now Rachel was a toddler and toddlers get into everything. There was also the possibility that perhaps in haste I had not put something exactly where I thought I had, and that's why it wasn't there when I went to retrieve it.

At an age where she was walking, but not yet talking, Rachel had a favorite ball. It was about eight inches in diameter, made of vinyl, but it was not a smooth sphere. Some rectangular chunks were cut out so that little fingers could easily grasp the ball with one hand. Still it was round and rolled easily.

One day Jack wanted the ball to play with Rachel, but he couldn't find it. I hadn't seen it for at least a couple of days. Since it was orange, it was easy to spot.

Jack made a thorough search of her room and the den, the play areas of the house. I helped in the search as it expanded to looking in more out-of-the-way places, but we failed to find it.

A couple mornings later Rachel woke up, I changed her diaper, and then put her down in the hallway while I went into the bathroom. She toddled down the hall into the den and within twenty seconds, she returned carrying the missing orange ball. Both Jack and I were incredulous! Where did she get that?

Obviously she had found her ball in the den, but the real question was, "How did it get there in plain view?" We had no explanation. We knew it was nowhere in sight the night before when we turned out the lights and went to bed. The next morning it was the first thing Rachel spied.

As time went on, not being able to find something became routine, but for me it was never normal. I'm not a careless, disorganized person. I tend to put things in the same place every time, and when something was not where I *knew* I'd put it, it would bug me.

For example, I had a set of six placemats, but unless we had guests, only two or three were used daily, and the clean ones stayed in a basket. One day after laundering the soiled ones, I went to switch them out with those in the basket. Strange. I counted five, not six. I recounted. Still five. I searched linen drawers and behind furniture, but I could only account for five placemats.

For several weeks, every time I did laundry, I would recount those placemats and feel like an idiot. Where was the sixth one? Then one day I counted and lo and behold! There were six! I counted them several times to be sure, and there was no denying that the stray placemat had rejoined its companions. Now I really felt like an idiot! Who put it there? What was going on? In retrospect, if I'd thought, "What in hell is going on here?" perhaps I would have more quickly reached the truth.

Often there were multiple items I couldn't find, and because their unexplained absence disrupted my sense of order, I'd make a list entitled, "things that are missing". When an item was located, I'd cross it off. Sometimes things were missing for so long that eventually I completely forgot about them. I pretty much stopped asking Jack if he knew where something was because he never did, and I was afraid I was beginning to sound a tad crazy, obsessing over misplaced things of little intrinsic value.

Then the day arrived when something of importance to Jack disappeared. My husband could not find his checkbook. He thought he'd put it on a particular shelf of the bookcase where he'd placed it many times. He quizzed me about moving it, which I hadn't done. Every evening after work he'd resume his search, looking in jacket pockets, pants pockets, checking every drawer of the desk and dresser, and finally he removed half the books on our large bookcase, but no checkbook.

Remember we were living in the pre-PC era, back when one had to rely on his check register and his monthly bank statement for his account balance. Debit cards did not yet exist, so if one did not use credit or cash, one paid by check, and Jack wrote lots of checks. Yes, he had the next sequence of new checks, but he was quite frustrated at losing his handwritten record of transactions going back three or four months.

If I had written down in a journal all these incidents, I could say with greater accuracy exactly how much time elapsed before the missing checkbook was located. Now I wish I had kept a journal.

I think perhaps it was months before I had need of a seldom-used cooking pot. Crouched down, looking into the dimly lit recesses of a kitchen cabinet, I discovered the checkbook against the back wall behind some pans. What was lost had been found, but instead of thinking that another mystery had been solved, we were left with more unanswered questions. How could a checkbook have traveled from a high shelf on a bookcase to a low shelf inside the kitchen cabinets?

As I stated, I didn't keep a written record of those incidents that impacted me at that time. During the writing of this manuscript, God brought back the memory of events in detail that surprised me, especially since I hadn't pondered these things in more than twenty years.

Another incident that I am quite sure about is this: I had four small Tupperware glasses—blue, green, yellow, and orange. The blue one disappeared. *At least two years later* I found it in my mailbox. This blue drinking glass was not at all dirty or scuffed. It was in mint condition, looking much newer than the other three. Clearly it had not been outdoors somewhere, subjected to the elements, but where had it been?

You may have heard of the occasional news account of a letter or package reaching its destination twenty or thirty years after it was mailed. You can imagine the disbelief of the recipient when he finds such a letter in his mailbox. However, this was not a long-lost envelope. It was a drinking glass, and it was in the mailbox! My mind failed to produce a plausible explanation.

After showing it to Jack, I stacked it in the cabinet with the other three glasses. Within a week it was gone again, and I haven't seen it since. As for the other three durable, oft-used glasses, they should be included in a testimonial to Tupperware. Not only do I still have them, but my grandchildren drink from them.

The reason I have written about these minor events is to demonstrate how spirits can create some havoc and do some tormenting in ways most of us would not suspect. Right now some of you are recalling little things which you've not been able to understand or explain, but in your spirit you've known something was amiss.

When God removed my blinders, I realized that most of the things that had happened were for the purpose of creating doubt. I started doubting myself, questioning myself, and wondering if it was the situation that was crazy, or was it me. These situations also caused me to waste time and energy that could have gone to better use. Once expended, those commodities can't be retrieved.

How or why did this happen? Matthew 12 refers to evil spirits occupying a man's house. While this refers to a physical body, and not a man-made structure, I don't think it's a stretch to connect spirits to actual dwelling places. Isn't that the assumption behind haunted houses? We've seen the movies. Someone dies, often violently, and that person's spirit is so disturbed or outraged by its unseemly demise, that it hangs around its earthly home for a hundred years tormenting unsuspecting, innocent homeowners.

In my situation I believe that the spirit or spirits simply came with the house. Why they originally made the house their home is anyone's guess. When we bought the house, unseen occupants came with it. Now *that's* something a realtor is unlikely to reveal.

"The seller is leaving all appliances, window treatments, and oh yes, all spirits that have attached themselves to the property."

The solution was easy. We used the same authority Jesus gave to his disciples. We commanded those tormenting spirits to leave. That house belonged to the Lord and He'd made us stewards over it. Any spirit that refused to bow to the Lord Jesus had no right to live in His house. We anointed the doorposts and windows of our home with oil as we consecrated the dwelling to God. When we first moved in, we had not known to do that. Following prayer and anointing, the spirits departed, and a new sense of peace and security came to abide in our home and in our hearts. What's the evidence? There were no further mysterious disappearances.

Taking it a step farther, might we extrapolate that if a spirit chooses to reside in one type of property, then might it not reside in any type of property? How many times have you heard or said, "I practically live in my car."? When we bought a used station wagon to meet the needs of our growing family, we got a rider that was not included in the deal.

Commonly, infants are quickly lulled to sleep by the movement of a vehicle. Some of you may have strapped your babies in car seats and driven around for no other purpose than to just calm them or put them to sleep.

By age two to three months, I noticed that car riding seemed to have the opposite effect upon my baby boy. Of course I tried to figure out what could be wrong so that I could fix it. Babies crying for more than a few minutes always cause me to tense up, but babies crying in the confines of a car when I'm helpless to pick them up can be extremely distracting.

I was certain that his crying wasn't a hunger issue or a comfort issue. When the efforts of his sisters failed to pacify him, and when we were still miles from our destination, it wasn't a pleasant drive for any of us. I began noticing that even on shorter car trips, say fifteen minutes, the likelihood of Spencer getting fussy seemed to be increasing.

Even before his birth I had petitioned God to give me a baby that liked to ride in the car. If you reside in a small town, you might think that's an unusual request. If you live in a sprawling metropolitan area, you immediately identify with my prayer. With three children, it was rare that a day passed without some reason to load them into a vehicle and set out for somewhere. So other than praying that this phase would pass quickly and that Spencer would adapt, I had no idea what else to do.

One afternoon we'd gone to Rachel's weekly vision therapy session. School was out for the summer so baby Spencer must have been five or six months old. On the return trip, we'd been in the car maybe five minutes max and were approaching the on-ramp to the interstate. Suddenly the crying starts, and I'm thinking, "There's just no reason for this. I can't listen to these wails for another twenty-five minutes." While I was quite frustrated, the girls had become so accustomed to his fussing that they continued with their chatter.

With absolutely no forethought I heard myself say, "I'm speaking to whatever spirits may be in this car." The crying shut off like a faucet!

Apparently I had a listening audience, so I kept talking, and now I was riled.

"You have no right to be in this car. Stop tormenting this child, in the name of Jesus! Spencer belongs to the Lord, this car belongs to the Lord, and it can no longer be your home. In Jesus' name, get out of here NOW and don't come back!"

I don't know who was more surprised to hear those words—me or the tormenting spirits! I started praising God and laughing while marveling more with every passing mile that the crying had not resumed! Within minutes, Spencer fell asleep and from that day forward, my baby rode peacefully in that car everywhere we went.

Looking back, I suppose I thought that infants were just too young to draw the attention of spirits, and that children would be walking and talking before demons would start messing with them. How naive I was!

Since 1973, a primary mission of Satan has been to kill babies in the womb. Satan obtained authority from the US Supreme Court who arbitrarily decided when life begins and whose life has more value—the baby's or the mother's.

Those babies who exit the womb safely continue to be targets of the enemy. If the parents are devoted to serving the Lord, those babies may be even larger targets because the devil knows that God has a destiny ordered for every family member.

Below I am listing some essential points for prayerful consideration:

1. Whether or not you are knowledgeable or have awareness of the spirit world does not prevent spirits from being active in your environment. If you have an "ignorance is bliss" or "what I don't know can't hurt me" attitude, then your thinking is foolish and sad. You cannot begin to be the overcoming conqueror by ignoring your foe and staying ignorant of his tactics. In fact, keeping you completely ignorant is one of Satan's best ploys.

2. God's protection is available to every believer, including those who are wearing spiritual blindfolds. I am a prime example. Although I had huge gaps in my spiritual foundation, the Lord provided divine aid when it was needed. Truly He watches over those who love Him.

3. What God desires is a heart that seeks Him fully, someone who is willing to take off his blindfold, open his spiritual eyes and ears, and who does not rely on his own understanding.

After reading this chapter on the spiritual battle which is being waged for your children, it is my hope that, at the very least, your level of awareness has risen. Do you believe that God has supplied us with every tool we need to live as His disciples? If so, then why is it difficult to believe He has supplied us with the tools we need to be guardian parents?

Indeed He has! Our job is to learn what the tools are and how to use them. Of what value are tools that remain in the toolbox? A tool is useful only to the extent that it is used.

5 The Sin of Rebellion

As previously stated, the legacy of Adam is that mankind is born with a bent to sin, and being good is against human nature. The sin that reared its ugly head in the Garden of Eden is still raging today. Its name is rebellion. We want to do what we want to do. That's a nutshell summary. Universally, we earthlings don't like anyone telling us what we should or should not do. As Americans living in democracy, I believe this self-determination thinking is even more pervasive.

Our rebelliousness has roots in the devil himself. The most beautiful of heaven's angels, Lucifer made the conscious choice to stop submitting to God's authority. He wanted to be in charge; then he fomented rebellion among other angels by persuading them to follow his leadership in the most foolish coup attempt of all time. An intelligent being, Satan realized he couldn't pull off the rebellion by himself, but he failed to recognize the idea was doomed and that there would be severe consequences. Rather than ascending to a throne above the Most High, he and his cohorts were evicted from heaven and cast down to the pit of the earth. (Isaiah 14:12–15 NIV)

Why didn't God just wipe out those rebellious angels right then and there? He certainly had the power to do it, and it would have made the world much less complicated.

God's plan for the future included creation in His own image, and so He made a bold move. He included free will—the ability to make choices—as part of the human makeup. Although it was within His power to program only "do-the-right-thing" messages in us, He took a risk and programmed in us the gamut of possibilities from "totally evil" to "completely selfless". While this made a Nero and a Hitler possible, it also allowed for a Mother Teresa.

The question in the heart of a loving parent is "How can I help my child to overcome his rebellious nature? Is it even possible?" There *are* ways we can counteract a rebellious nature at a young age. The first involves teaching and practicing obedience until it becomes habitual. It is a process that requires diligence and commitment.

Parents, you must be serious about whatever you tell your children to do. If you are not serious, if you really don't care whether or not they obey, then you are merely making a suggestion or request. If you intend for them to obey, if you mean business, then it is a command. Commands aren't necessarily loud and forceful; they may be quietly spoken. It's the follow-through that determines your effectiveness.

Imagine the disastrous results if a General offered suggestions instead of commands to his troops. Chaos and calamity would ensue as everyone did what they thought was best. Homes across America are filled with chaos and calamity because parents lack the backbone to 1. Give some orders and 2. Follow through and see that they are obeyed. Some of you don't want to be seen as the General giving your diminutive troops their marching orders. Where is the leadership if it doesn't reside with the parents? Who has given you permission to abdicate your God-given assignment?

If you want to soften your orders a bit by using the word "please", that's fine as long as both you and your troops (children) understand that you are just modeling courtesy. Stated politely, your request is still a command and obedience is mandatory.

For your children to truly know that you are serious, you have to be willing to be the enforcer, even if it means feeling like you are the bad guy in your home movie. Most marriages have one partner who is more reticent about enforcing rules and following through, and the two of you will have to work it out privately. Moms, you don't want to be a "wait until your father comes home" parent. If you are, your kids will exploit your weakness to the max. To be an enforcer requires extra time and extra effort, but the character that is being built in your child makes your time and effort worthwhile.

Disobedience brings consequences is a Biblical principle made starkly clear in the lives of nearly every major patriarch, king, and the nation of Israel itself. From Adam to Abraham to Moses to David, God demonstrates that sin reaps discipline while faithfulness and obedience bring rewards.

This is a life lesson for everyone, and the earlier a child sees that this is the way the world works, the happier and more successful he'll be. If a child learns that sometimes there's a consequence and sometimes there's not, initially he'll be a little confused. As time goes on, their rebellious natures, especially of strong-willed children, cause them to risk disobeying. After all, there's a possibility they will get away with it!

Of course there are times that God gives us grace rather than the full penalty of what we deserve, and certainly we should demonstrate grace in dealing with our own children as well. However, we need to point out exactly what we are doing—that we are extending grace to them. We also need to make clear our expectations regarding future situations. Be sure they know that grace will not always abound.

Avoid the traps of negotiating and explaining, especially with younger children. If you negotiate and explain, the message they receive is that it's okay to argue and okay to question what they've been told. That's NOT the message you want to send. Without verbalizing "because I'm the mommy/daddy, that's why", you can still internalize it, for this is the necessary mindset.

As a child grows, negotiation regarding a rule may at times be appropriate, and that's different than negotiation regarding obedience. For example, a ten year old may request his bedtime moved from 8:30

to 9:00 on school nights. If the child wakes up easily in the mornings, it might be workable to allow him another thirty minutes before "lights out". On the other hand, if you practically pry him from his sheets in the mornings, then going to bed later is likely not a wise move. Explain what behavior changes you need to see demonstrated regularly before you are willing to change the bedtime.

As adults with God-given authority, why do we allow ourselves to be lured into believing that we need to justify to our kids everything we say or do? We don't! When kids ask questions, it is often a procrastination ploy because as long as you're explaining the "why", the longer they can delay obeying.

Setting Boundaries

It is astounding how many parents are reluctant to set boundaries and enforce them. I think the primary reason is because they are thinking of the immediate present rather than thinking long-term. In the financial world, brokers advise us on long-term investments. They focus on results years into the future. As parents we have to look beyond today and this week and focus on the long-term results we want to see in our children. This is never truer than when parenting your teen. Seeing only the present will drive you crazy. You have to keep your eyes on the future goal.

In regard to boundaries, let me share an example that encompasses both visible and unseen parameters. A boy's love affair with his personal transportation starts early. Spencer was ready for his training wheels to be removed from his bike at age four. That's when it dawned on me that those extra little wheels had served a purpose beyond helping him keep his balance. They had also provided restriction, both physically and psychologically. Once those training wheels were off, he felt free as a bird, and he wanted to fly.

Now birds may not need boundaries, but boys on bikes do. We

moved to a new neighborhood when he was in first grade. In the beginning we told him he could ride just from corner to corner on the street in front of our house. Then we granted permission to ride around the block, but only during the low-traffic daylight hours.

Spencer was quick to push for more territory. If it was okay to ride around the block the house faced, then why not the block behind the house? Another lesson: Kids are never content with the amount of freedom they are given. They will *always* want more!

He became friends with two boys who both lived on the farthest street of the subdivision. By this time he was seven, and at first we began allowing him to walk to their houses. Of course, he wasn't happy with this arrangement because once he got to their street, a long cul-de-sac, he didn't have a bike to ride with his buddies.

In order for Spencer to have the privilege of cycling with his friends and for me to be comfortable in regard to safety, I chose to inconvenience myself a bit. Sometimes I would load the bike in the back of the car and drive him. Of course, later I'd have to pick him up. His friends' parents never offered to bring Spencer and his bicycle home, and it wasn't their responsibility to do that. For us it was a solution that worked.

At age nine we felt more confident about increasing his boundaries for riding throughout the entire neighborhood, but now a new rule needed to be established. "Don't go anywhere without telling someone where you're going."

Both his sisters had babysitting clients in the neighborhood, and over time we'd become at least slightly acquainted with lots of nearby residents. He had many chances for interaction as he rode up and down streets, and that's why following a simple, straightforward rule became a challenge for my social son.

Except for breaking the "don't throw balls in the house" rule, Spencer violated "tell us where you're going" more than any other rule. Although he'd lose his bike-riding privilege for longer and longer periods of time, he just seemed to miss the point.

He'd see someone in a yard with a dog, and he'd stop and play with the dog for half an hour. He'd say he was going to play at Al's house. Three hours later I'd call for him to come home for dinner and I'd get the answering machine. When Al's family left their house, Spencer had gone to Chris' house, but had not called to tell me the new location. I can't even guess how many times a scenario like that played out. Sometimes I'd have to make several phone calls or even drive around looking for him. It wasn't that he was going somewhere I'd disapprove. I don't think he was deliberately not calling. He just wasn't focused on obedience to the point of intentionally making a phone call.

I'll never forget the evening when I'd either phoned or gone to the door of every house where I thought he might possibly be. He had not taken his bike, it was not summer, it was dark, and I hadn't found him. Naturally, I was mad because once again he was not where he was supposed to be. What if he'd been abducted? Then I'd feel guilty at being mad when I should have been concerned. We decided that Jack would drive the neighborhood one more time, and then we were calling the police.

Returning home at the same time, the incident had a happy ending as Jack and Spencer met up with each other in the garage. Boy, did we want to hear an explanation! The story went like this:

On his way home from Chris' house, he saw a kid shooting baskets. He'd never talked to this younger boy before, didn't even know his name. The two of them got involved in playing basketball, and when it started getting dark, the mother invited Spencer to come inside, where the boys began playing video games. When dinner was about to be served, the mother politely suggested that Spencer leave and come back another day.

Incredible! He was having fun and making a new friend while his parents were forming a search and rescue team!

Some of you are thinking this makes a good case for why eleven year olds need cell phones. I completely disagree. Cell phones do not teach responsibility. Parents teach responsibility. Cell phones do not teach responsibility. Parents teach responsibility. Keep repeating these two sentences until the message has been fully absorbed.

In addition to the "whereabouts" violation, Spencer failed to return home before dark, plus he had gone inside a house at the invitation of a stranger! Clearly we were failing in our parenting. His consequences included getting grounded for two weeks, which meant he was prohibited from all biking and from playing at anyone's house—in our neighborhood or elsewhere.

Remember that I said that you have to think long term? What I kept thinking was, "Until he obeys the bike rules, until he consistently lets us know where he is, there is NO WAY that kid is getting car keys!"

6 Preying On the Innocent

In 1 Peter 5:8 the Word tells us that Satan himself is like a prowling lion, looking for someone to devour. We know that in the animal kingdom that predators, such as the big cats, intelligently and purposefully select their prey. They single out the smallest, the weakest, the wounded, the one who is on the fringe or wandering beyond the rest of the herd.

Satan's tactics are no different. He goes after the one whose spiritual defenses are weak, the one who is distracted by everyday life and whose guard is down. He targets those who have separated themselves from the body, who refrain from regularly joining corporate worship, those who are neglecting to strengthen themselves through prayer and by feeding on the Word.

If the enemy sees you as a weak Christian, rather than a strong one, then you are marked as easy prey. By making choices that are not in your spiritual best interest, you may unwittingly invite an attack.

Another way in which the devil insinuates himself into a believer's life is through sins of the flesh. A believer who allows himself to become entrapped in such a lifestyle is giving the enemy territory that should belong to the Lord. Sinful practices would include drunkenness, all addictions, lying, stealing, or sexual sins such as adultery, fornication, and homosexuality. Once Satan thinks he has a rightful claim on a person due to habitual sin, he becomes ruthless in his desire to take ever-greater control.

It is important to draw a clear distinction between adults and infants. While everyone is born with sin as part of their inherited nature, babies, of course, are incapable of making conscious decisions between right and wrong. If the devil goes prowling for those whose spiritual defenses are weak, then who is more defenseless and vulnerable than a tiny infant? Only a baby who is still inside the womb. Sadly, Satan does not exempt the innocent from becoming his targets.

Medical research continues to show that whatever a mother ingests—food, alcohol, drugs—directly affects her unborn child. Research also indicates that for all of us, our emotional state of being is reflected in our bodies. For the expectant mother those emotions—positive or negative— affect her developing baby.

What science has not yet provided is evidence that babies who are not loved and emotionally nurtured pre-birth will somehow sense it. Without facts to back me up, I'm going to say that it is my humble opinion that if a mother fails to establish a strong, loving bond with the baby she is carrying, that baby will be adversely affected. He/she will lack a crucial component in their emotional fabric.

What if the mother decides to give up her baby for adoption? No matter how valid her reasons may be, when all the circumstances are stripped away, what remains is abandonment and rejection. It is the perfect situation for a spirit of rejection to establish itself in a defenseless infant. Over time, if unaddressed, that spirit of rejection will hinder the child from receiving the fullness of love being freely offered from the adoptive parents. It serves as a filter screen, altering or blocking the positive messages, making it difficult for the child to really "get" deep down that he is one hundred percent wanted, loved, and accepted into the family.

Let's create a mental picture describing how children feel if they've experienced some form of abandonment at a young age. Picture a child knocking on a door. A voice inside says, "Come in!" The child heard the reply, but keeps knocking. The voice is closer now and repeats the invitation to enter. Still the child continues to knock, unresponsive to the beckoning voice, until finally the adult opens wide the door and extends his arm, saying "come on in!" Yet the child hesitates, unsure if he is really welcome.

Why? He longs for full admittance and acceptance, but is doubtful it will happen because that has not been his past experience. Until someone has *experienced* rejection, he cannot *anticipate* rejection.

At a time when adoptions were carried out quietly, behind closed doors, and when some slight degree of shame was attached, the atmosphere was ripe for rejection to flourish. The cultural tone of that era dictated that adopted babies be a close biological match to the parents. In the 1950's, no Caucasian parents considered adopting a child of Asian or Negro heritage, and vice versa. Blonde, blue-eyed parents wanted blonde, blue-eyed babies.

Difficult as it may be to imagine now that open adoptions abound, another aspect of an earlier era was secrecy. Parents commonly did not reveal to children that they had been adopted. Yet without even knowing this vital information, many children grew to adulthood sensing that they were "different" or "didn't fit" with the rest of their family. In short, these children felt as if they really didn't belong. This is how a spirit of rejection operates. It caused them to see themselves as outsiders among the very people who loved them most.

Rejection by a biological mother has a profound affect. In the animal kingdom, when a dog or cat rejects a newborn puppy or kitten, it will die without human intervention. Thankfully human babies in the US are typically born in an environment where immediate physical care is offered, and professional caregivers do their best to insure healthy lives.

When a human mother decides to relinquish her rights, she is declining to accept her parental role and is passing the responsibility to someone else. No matter how valid her reasons, and even if this truly is in the baby's best interest, the door is opened for the spirit of rejection to enter.

The earlier in a child's life that this spirit is dealt with, the less effect it will have on his personality. When the child starts displaying signs of insecurity, and if parents are clueless about what is going on, they will treat the symptom instead of the cause. The word of God gives the adoptive parents the authority to command that spirit to stop tormenting His child.

Will the rejection spirit depart immediately? Perhaps not, but your persistence must outlast the persistence of the entrenched spirit. Know that it *will* depart, so don't give up until you see evidence in terms of behavior change.

Without doubt the most effective tool a parent can pull from his spiritual tool kit is prayer. The effectiveness of your prayer is maximized when it is spoken aloud over your sleeping child. The reason is because when sleeping, your child offers no physical resistance.

You may recall that when I spoke grace to Julia the third time, she tried to wriggle out of my arms. When a child is sleeping, your full attention can be focused on what is transpiring spiritually, and physical control or restraint is not an issue.

How can I know what spirits are affecting my child? Trust the Holy Spirit to guide you, but any obvious sin that you see *repeatedly* has a corresponding spirit. For example, if your child seems to be having a problem with obeying despite your best, consistent disciplinary efforts, then disobedience may have established itself. A stronger form of disobedience is defiance. "Disobedience" doesn't do what he's told. "Defiance" refuses to do it or chooses to do just the opposite.

Brothers and sisters, why would you allow these sins to take root and flourish in your children? Does your child argue and then argue some more? Then cast out the spirit of argumentation, so that your "no" will be "no."

Here's a sample prayer over a sleeping child:

Father, I thank you for the gift of my son Michael. Thank you for entrusting his precious life to me, and I believe you will equip me to be the dad that You want me to be, and the dad that Michael needs me to be.

I take my authority as his father directly from You, my Heavenly Father. I bind the spirits of rebellion and disobedience in the name of Jesus. Spirits of rebellion and disobedience, you must release Michael because he is God's child, created by Him and in His image. No longer can you have influence over him, and you have no right to dwell in this house. Jesus is Lord of this house and Lord of this family.

Keep praying until you have cast out every spirit God brings to mind, and until you believe the spiritual work is being accomplished according to the Father's will.

Now flood Michael with your Holy Spirit and with the fruit of the Spirit. Fill him with your love, joy, peace, patience, kindness, goodness, gentleness, and self control. Place within him the desire to obey his parents, teachers, and all those in authority. May Your will be done in Michael's life every day. Amen.

Let me say there is no formula. There is no single "right" way to pray over your child. I can't stress enough that you need to have your own spiritual life in order, and then be led by the Spirit as to how and when to pray. If you do, then you will see results. Will they last forever? Not necessarily. We are all sinners who make choices that are against the nature and will of God, and when we make the same bad choice over and over, we open that spiritual door that allows unclean/ungodly spirits to gain entrance.

James 4:7 says resist the devil and he will flee from you. It doesn't say ignore the devil and hope he will leave you alone. On the contrary, Satan is an opportunist—always looking for a chance to enlarge his territory.

To me it is noteworthy that Jesus did not use his supernatural power when dealing with Satan. As the greatest of superheroes, he could have stretched forth his hand and zapped the devil with a lightning bolt. Instead he used the Word of God which is a weapon sharper than a double-edge sword.

Following his baptism, Jesus fasted forty days and nights in the wilderness. Matthew 4 records three specific ways Satan tempted him.

First, Satan tempted Christ to break the fast, turn stones into bread, and eat. Next he asked Jesus to test God's protection by throwing himself from the pinnacle of the temple. Finally the devil offered power and rulership over kingdoms if Christ would worship him.

Jesus responded to every temptation by quoting the law in Deuteronomy. "Man does not live on bread alone, but on every word that comes from the mouth of God." Strike one. "Do not put the Lord your God to the test." Strike two. "Worship the Lord your God, and serve him only." Strike three and the devil was literally out of there. Matthew says Satan departed and angels came to attend to Jesus.

If you think you might be under spiritual attack, stop and ask the Holy Spirit if you are. Not everything happens due to spiritual warfare. From living in a fallen world, we see and experience bad things happening to righteous people. If the Spirit confirms that you are indeed experiencing an attack, pray for God's power to enable you to resist.

By following Jesus' example and using the Word, you can put the devil in his rightful place. "You have already won a victory... because the Spirit who lives in you is greater than the spirit who lives in the world." (I John 4:4 NLT) Use situation appropriate verses and always speak out loud because only God is omniscient and knows your thoughts. Satan doesn't know what you're thinking until you tell him. The Lord is on your side, and if He is for you, then it doesn't matter who may come against you. In the midst of battle we must remember that just as surely as Jesus was victorious over death, we are victorious over the enemy of our souls. Live as a victor!

7 The Truth Behind Fears and Lies

In Strong's Concordance there are more than four hundred entries for "fear" and its variations. One category for fear means the reverential awe we should have for Jehovah God. This type of fear is highly encouraged. The other fear category relates to being afraid. Frequently this Biblical usage is followed by the word "not". *Fear not.*

God did not pre-wire our brains for fear, nor did He weave fear into our DNA. Fears are learned in two ways: through our own experiences or they have been taught to us. No one is born with a fear of heights, fear of falling, fear of the dark, fear of dogs, etc. Fears are learned.

It's a *lack* of fear that allows children to find themselves in truly dangerous situations, where they rightfully should be afraid, but because it's a new experience, they don't know they should be scared.

One way to learn fear is by personal experience or through the experience of someone else. For example, a child can develop a fear of falling after climbing to the top of the jungle gym and toppling off. It's a little less bruising if he sees another child fall off and then makes the connection that he also could fall.

Let's consider that fears are also learned by modeling or teaching. Children seem to naturally mimic and will imitate adults who are regularly in their environment. Using smoking as a prime example, it's no surprise that studies indicate a majority of cigarette smokers had at least one parent or adult in the household who was a smoker. They simply copied what they had seen modeled and ignored all admonitions to the contrary.

We also learn to fear by someone teaching us that we should be fearful. Children who seem scared of every little thing have learned those behaviors from a well-meaning parent or caregiver. As adults we can easily envision the worst case scenario, but do we really want to live our lives based on worst case scenarios? If we are always preparing for the worst, then how do we expect the best?

Referring to my jungle gym example, the very worst case scenario would be that a child falls off, lands on his head, and dies. The next-to-worst possibility is that a bone is broken or there are internal injuries. Even if a child is old enough to understand these severe consequences, the wise parent isn't going to stand there and say, "Do you know that if you fall, you could break your arm?" That's instilling fear rather than confidence. Should his climbing be restricted on the basis of what *might* happen?

Here's how I would handle the situation with my own children. If they desired to climb, I would allow them to attempt it. I would be physically close enough to supervise and give any needed instructions. I'd also give encouragement and praise after they had successfully reached the top and more praise after they reached the ground. If they discovered for themselves that it was too difficult or too scary, I'd help them down in the safest way and tell them they could try again later.

What I would NOT do is give lots of warnings like, "You could get hurt doing that!" I would tell them "be careful" only once and they would know I meant it. Someone please tell me the value of saying "don't fall". No one ever *intends* to fall! Saying "don't fall" shifts the child's focus from climbing to falling.

Allowing them to climb promotes independence and self-confidence. Pointing out the dangers and repeating "be careful" a dozen times promotes fear. Even if they need some help getting back to the ground, they will have learned from the experience and will feel better about themselves than if they'd never tried.

From a common sense point of view, remember that we're talking about a jungle gym— an apparatus built for the purpose of climbing. Not only is that key to safety, but it's key in our conversation. Would I allow a five year old to climb on top of an SUV? No, because SUV's weren't built for that purpose, and I would consider it too dangerous. Would I allow a twelve year old to do it? Again, I say no. While safety is a lesser issue for a twelve year old, now I would be more concerned about possible damage to the vehicle.

Here's my point. Too many cautions and restrictions will serve to instill a spirit of fear, and the result will be a child who is afraid of new experiences, afraid of unfamiliar situations, and lacking in confidence.

Do any of these descriptions fit your children? Do any of them fit *you*? If as a parent, this describes your own tendencies, then unless you break free yourself, your child (the imitator) will learn to operate from a base of fear.

Moms are the biggest culprits. Almost every clingy, fearful child was taught to be that way through the attitudes, words, and behavior conveyed by the mother. Whether she intends to or not, she is forming a child who is just like her.

The Book of Job begins with a description of a man who was blameless and upright, who feared God (with the reverence type of fear) and shunned evil. We read that Job was blessed with seven sons and three daughters, a large number of servants, and herds numbering in the thousands. He was among the richest of the rich.

Verses 4–5 tell an interesting tale. Job's children liked to party and took turns being the host. Apparently these parties lasted more than just a few hours. The scripture says that when a period of feasting had run its course, Job's regular custom was to sacrifice a burnt offering for each of his children, thinking, "Perhaps my children have sinned and cursed God in their hearts."

The rest of chapter one relates God's conversation with Satan and the calamities that ensued by Satan's hand. Imagine Job's shock upon hearing of his murdered servants, his stolen herds, and how fire had fallen from the sky to consume flocks and shepherds alike. Before he could grasp the enormity of it all, he learns the fate of his children. While they were feasting and drinking wine at the oldest brother's house, a category four storm collapses the house, killing all ten children.

Now let's skip to Job 3:25. It reads, "What I always feared has happened to me. What I dreaded has come true." (NLT)

I think Job's biggest fear was the same fear that God-fearing parents have today. First, he was afraid that the Lord was not a priority in the lives of his offspring, as evidenced by their sinful lifestyles. Second, Job may have feared that the sins of his sons would lead to their destruction. His worry and concern prompted him to offer sacrifices on their behalf. It isn't difficult to imagine a slew of devastating circumstances that can occur in an atmosphere of drunken revelry. These adult children literally left themselves defenseless to any attack that the enemy would bring.

I too, like Job, set myself up by allowing a specific fear to take root in my heart. Each of us has heard/read/or been touched by a tragedy that for whatever reason has made an indelible impression.

Nearly thirty years ago I heard such a story related by Kay Arthur of Precept Ministries. She told of a young mother who accidentally drove her car over her young child while backing out the driveway and described that mother's anguish as she held her child's lifeless body. She spoke of a horror like few of us will ever face, and now I can't recall Kay's purpose for telling it. You see, before she had even finished the teaching, my mind had already begun drawing conclusions and making decisions.

At the time of my motherhood calling, I had been employed as an automobile claims adjustor for several years. It was my job to understand how and why accidents happened. Now with a little three year old of my own, it was very easy for me to envision situations where such an awful accident could occur.

My heart broke for this mother. My rational mind of an insurance adjuster told me she was "at fault", and for me that only compounded the grief. I remember sharing the story with my husband and friends, and I definitely wondered aloud, *"How will she ever be able to forgive herself? If that happened to me, I would always live with the knowledge that even though it was an accident, it would still be my fault, and I would never be able to forgive myself for my mistake."*

This woman's tragedy so impacted me that I determined to never find myself in that situation. From that day forward, I *never, ever,* backed out of our carport without absolutely knowing that Rachel was either safe inside the house or securely held in her daddy's arms.

Now fast forward four or five years, and I am a carpool driver taking children to a Christian school. In our full-sized sedan, four children squeezed into the backseat, and two sat in front with me. Sometimes in their haste to exit the car, one or even both of the back doors would be left open. Then I'd have to unbuckle, get out, and perhaps walk to the right side of the car to shut the rear door. I found the minor inconvenience slightly annoying.

This particular day I was focused on looking over my right shoulder in case a reminder to close the door was needed. As I looked ahead of me, about to put the car in "drive" and pull forward, I noticed a tall woman begin walking toward me. My impression at the time was that she had been speaking with the driver of the car several yards ahead, and now as she moved nearer, she appeared to be looking down at my left front tire. I was wondering, "Does she want to tell me something? Is my tire low on air?"

Then the stranger extended her hand downward, and when she raised it, she was grasping Rachel's hand. Dear God! I quickly jumped out to learn what had happened. Rachel had slipped on the gravel parking lot, falling unseen by me, right in front of the car. Except for some minor scrapes, she was unhurt and walked to her classroom.

Halfway in shock, I know I said, "thank you" to the stranger who was already walking away. She smiled, but she didn't say a word, and that was fine with me. I did not need her to point out my nearly fatal mistake.

As I got back into the car and slowly drove through the parking lot, I was inwardly shaking and my mind was racing. *"I could have run over her. I would have run over her. I almost ran over my own child. Thank you, Lord, for saving her. Thank you, thank you."*

I ached as the weight of the unthinkable permeated my numb mind. Gradually the shock subsided, and I was forced to admit that **what I had feared most had nearly happened.**

Of all the close calls that a child can have, why did we experience this particular one? My mind searched for an explanation because somehow I sensed that the near accident was not entirely accidental. There was a lesson to be learned, and I was determined to learn it.

What I believe is that because I had allowed my mind to dwell repeatedly on this exact type of tragedy, and because I had *verbalized my thoughts and feelings* numerous times, the evil one who hates us looked for an opportunity to cause devastation to my family.

All ten of Job's children were killed in one fell swoop because God allowed it. In my situation the devil didn't succeed because clearly there was divine intervention. No question about it.

While I sought to spot that unfamiliar woman at carpool drop-off or parent meetings, I never saw her again. I am completely convinced that she was an angel who needed to take human form. Whether she was Rachel's guardian every day before that and every day since, only the Lord knows. What I do know is on that particular day she fulfilled her assignment of protecting my daughter's life. If I recognize her in heaven, and if angels have actual wings, hers will get compressed when I give her my biggest hug.

Undoubtedly, Satan has a field day with our fears, and that's why our confession needs to be faith-based, not fear-based. A fear-based confession is focused on our lack. A faith-based confession is focused on

God's promises to supply all our needs. A fear-based confession believes the doctor's prognosis. A faith-based confession says that by His stripes I am healed. A fear-based confession says, "That's too difficult. I can't do it." A faith-based confession says, "I can do everything through the power of the Lord Jesus who gives me His strength."

Father of Lies

"When he (the devil) lies, he speaks his native language, for he is a liar and the father of lies." (John 8:44 NIV) What does the devil lie about? Anything that suits his purpose, and for sure, he always has a strategy.

If frequency is an indicator, one of Satan's favorite strategies is to tell us lies about ourselves. To some he says that we are more than we really are. Satan says you are okay just the way you are. Actually, you're more than okay. You're very special. You deserve VIP status. By elevating our self-esteem, he diminishes our need for a Savior.

To others the devil's message is that we are less than most everyone else. He says we will never be good enough to deserve the pure love of a holy God, and no matter how hard we try, sin will always ensnare us. Satan tells us that we will never be conquerors.

Another of the enemy's primary strategies is to convince the world that God is less than He really is. Again, the devil goes to extremes. He can paint God as distant and disinterested in mankind. Or he can paint God as so loving that He tolerates sin. Indeed, Satan has convinced many that what the Bible states as intolerable is now acceptable, and furthermore, it should be legal. My friends, God's thoughts do not evolve. Not only is He not a man that can lie or change his mind (Num. 23:19 NIV), but He is the same yesterday, today, and forever. (Heb. 13:8 NIV).

Indeed the father of lies has many children. You can spot them in the marketplace, in the classroom, and sadly, even in pulpits. We have elected them to positions of influence.

In John chapter 10, Jesus compares himself to a shepherd who knows his sheep and his sheep know him. The shepherd is willing to sacrifice his life for his precious sheep, for he considers each one to be valuable. The sheep recognize and respond to their shepherd's voice.

As the master of deception, Satan tries to pass himself off as a good shepherd. In reality, his purpose is to steal from the flock, or bring suffering and destruction. As followers of Christ, we all have targets on our backs. He wants to bring misery to God's children, and if he is able to steal or destroy the life of your child, then he has successfully brought down multiple targets with one arrow. If my car had rolled over my child, it would have killed her, but there are many ways to destroy a child's life while they are still living.

Appearing as a serpent in the Garden of Eden, Satan convinced Eve to believe a lie. She knew that God had said they were not to eat the fruit or even touch the tree that grew in the middle of the garden, or they would die.

"You will not surely die," the serpent replied. "For God knows that when you eat of it, your eyes will be opened, and you will be like God, knowing both good and evil." (Gen. 3:4-5 NIV)

It is my sincere hope that Eve didn't give in and agree immediately. I like to imagine that she argued a bit ("Yes, that *is* what God said") and that the crafty serpent wore down her defenses as he slowly led her ever closer to the forbidden tree until she finally resisted no more and reached out her hand to pick and taste the luscious fruit.

That's the way I visualize the scene in my head, but whatever manner in which the deed happened, the consequences were the same. Adam and Eve *would* die, and their spiritual death began the moment they disobeyed. However, the serpent had been telling the truth when he said their eyes would be opened to know good and evil, for verse seven states this is precisely what happened.

Thousands of years later the apostle Peter warns us, "Stay alert! Watch out for your great enemy, the devil. He prowls around like a roaring lion, looking for someone to devour." (I Peter 5:8 NLT) We surely do need to stay alert! Sometimes we can see or hear the enemy coming, but at other times, he's very quiet and subtle. Either way, his mission is the same: to steal, to kill, to destroy.

If a parent has his or her spiritual antennae extended, he or she will pick up on things that are not as they should be. Please trust and know that the Lord will bring it to awareness at just the right time.

One afternoon I was trying to get a brief nap on the couch. At age six or seven Rachel was very capable of playing quietly by herself. Anyway, you know how mothers nap—with one eye and one ear open.

I was aware that she was speaking softly as she engaged in some imaginary play, but I became alert when she spoke more sharply saying, "Be quiet, Shaggy."

Of course I knew who Shaggy was. He's the doofus, uh, main character, in the cartoon *Scooby Doo*. Rachel watched *Scooby Doo* episodes almost daily. Shaggy, his friends, and his dog solved mysteries. It was harmless entertainment.

Although I thought I'd clearly heard her, I inquired, "What did you just say?"

Rachel replied, "I told Shaggy to be quiet."

I asked, "Was Shaggy talking to you?"

"Yes."

"What was he saying?"

"He said I was dumb—that I didn't know anything."

Then I asked if she could see Shaggy in the room.

"Yes, he's right over there."

Now fully awake, that startling revelation led to a slew of more questions in which I learned that Shaggy came to our house often and he came alone—no Scooby or any of his buddies.

When I asked Rachel, "What else does Shaggy say to you?" I wasn't prepared to hear her say one of the verboten words.

"He calls me 'stupid'."

At that point I began to counteract those negative messages by telling her that she knew that what Shaggy said wasn't true. She was a very smart girl, and I did not want her to pay attention to anything Shaggy said.

Back then deliverance was a fairly new concept to me and my knowledge was very limited. It was no coincidence that my sovereign Father had just arranged that very same day for me to make the acquaintance of Rev. Tom Hodges, whose ministry was discernment of spirits and deliverance. Immediately I was on the phone to him, seeking his counsel.

Rev. Hodges explained to me that Shaggy was a familiar spirit. A familiar spirit is one that is known to the individual who sees it. Because the spirit visits frequently, the person grows accustomed to its presence and isn't frightened. In this instance, the spirit manifested in the already familiar form of a cartoon character, but more often the spirit will not be initially recognized. It is over time and repeated interactions that it becomes familiar. Rev. Hodges instructed me that as parents, we would need to exercise our authority over this spirit and bind it from harming our daughter.

Following his counsel, we waited until nighttime when Rachel was sleeping soundly. Then we commenced warfare at her bedside. As we prayed and ordered the demon to leave our house and to leave her alone, the purpose of the Shaggy spirit became evident to me. Shaggy wanted Rachel to become just like him! The names he called her described himself. Dumb. Stupid.

Furthermore, he was trying to make her a klutz, just like he is comically portrayed. I had noticed that Rachel sometimes seemed to trip or fall for no reason. In my ignorance I'd chalked it up to an awkward phase due to a growth spurt.

After our prayer, all clumsiness disappeared overnight! From that point, Rachel only tripped if there was an actual object in her path. She ran like a deer.

Once that fiendish spirit left her alone, my daughter very quickly forgot that it ever existed. A couple weeks later I wanted to make sure it hadn't popped up, so I asked her, "Have you seen Shaggy lately?" She seemed puzzled and unsure of what I meant. How amazing is that! God is so good! Needless to say, *Scooby Doo* never made another television appearance in our home.

Something that Tom Hodges told me stuck in my head, and while I was debating whether or not to include yet another personal story in this manuscript, there was a brief news account which prompts me to plunge in.

The report was about a toddler, not quite two years old, who had wandered out of his South Carolina home with the family dog, and had been missing overnight in a heavily wooded area. Thankfully the story had a happy ending as the next morning he was found about a half mile away. The dog was credited for keeping the little guy safe and warm.

The insight Rev. Hodges shared with me is this: Many of the children who have been reported missing are led away by spirits. Everyone assumes that they are always bodily abducted by an evil person, when it is often an evil spirit that leads the child into a dangerous situation.

For example, there are accounts of families who have been camping in remote areas, and a child vanishes. Clearly there were no pedophiles around waiting for the chance to snatch a victim. It was Rev. Hodges' belief that these children were lured away by a spirit.

There were two instances where my young son was led away from our home, but when they happened, I placed blame on our incorrigible cocker spaniel. The first instance was when Beau and Spencer, age three, were left unchaperoned in the front yard on a Saturday afternoon. Jack had come in to rest from yard work, and it was at least fifteen minutes before it occurred to either of us to check up on them. They weren't in our yard. Within a few minutes we had covered the houses on our street, calling both their names. Slightly panicked, we returned home to get the car keys so the search could be expanded.

Inside I heard the phone ringing. The woman on the line inquired if my dog was missing. She'd called the number on his tag. Oh, and there was a small boy with blonde hair that appeared to be accompanying the dog. Currently both dog and boy were in her backyard, and the child was playing on her swing set.

Jack jumped in the car to retrieve them from an adjoining neighborhood. What we surmised was that they wandered through an unfenced backyard on our street and just kept going until Spencer found a yard that attracted him to stop and play. Beau usually lived in our backyard, only occasionally privileged to spend time in the front, so his dog nature wanted to explore new territory.

Just five days later, Spencer was playing in our fenced backyard. Usually I let him into the yard via the door in the basement playroom. I always left the door ajar so he could come back in by himself whenever he wanted. When I went to check on him, he and Beau were gone, and the fence gate stood wide open. Here we go again.

I set off jogging up the street, calling their names. A neighbor told me she saw them five minutes earlier. Boy and dog were headed toward the very busy street which fed all the neighborhoods. My heart nearly stopped.

Arriving at that street, I had a long clear view of the sidewalks in both directions, and they weren't in sight. I crossed the street, entering a new development where townhomes were under construction. That's where I found them, among the two-by-fours, doing nothing in particular. Surprisingly, that day there were no workmen present.

I was shaken at the thought of the dangers that had been avoided. First, God had led them safely across a heavily trafficked thoroughfare. Second, the building site held potentially dozens of ways a small child could get hurt. With no workmen to steer him away, my son had come to no harm.

When we got home, I gave Spencer a spanking for letting the dog loose and for leaving the yard. The previous Saturday he had been warned he was *not* to go past the end of the driveway. I felt sure that if the dog had not left the yard, Spencer would not have left either, but my son had to understand that no matter what Beau did, he could not follow him.

That night at church I shared the story with a couple friends. They listened with wide eyes, looked at each other, then both started speaking. It was a *spirit* in the dog that had led Spencer into danger. Didn't I realize that? They had no doubts about where the blame should be placed.

Perhaps I am a slow learner because a spiritual explanation had not occurred to me. My natural mind wanted to place responsibility on an obstinate, willful dog who took advantage of a bit of freedom. Yet I knew their succinct assessment was correct.

So at home I obediently prayed over Beau, claiming that since his owners were themselves owned by Christ, no demons had the right to enter or influence him. Apparently it worked because after that, boy and dog did not set out on more adventures.

Reflecting on that South Carolina toddler, I am sure that the heat from the dog's body during the cold night was indeed a blessing, and that the dog's presence would have kept other animals at bay. However, I am equally sure that it was a spirit operating through the dog that initially led the child into the dark woods on that spring evening.

I have mentioned fear, lies, and deception as tactics the enemy employs against us. Another weapon he uses to his advantage is what I refer to as "the storms of life".

It should come as no surprise that the devil also tries to bring us down through situations with people we love dearly. Ask the boy whose world got rocked when his dad abandoned the family. Ask the girl who was molested by an adored uncle. Ask the jilted husband whose wife was lured by an internet "friend." Ask the wife whose husband and father of her children decides he's gay.

These are just a few examples of very deep wounds that loved ones can inflict. They shake each person to the core. Sometimes hearts become so hardened that it's very difficult for faith to ever take root. Even where faith in God may pre-exist, that person's faith may not be strong enough to prevail. Satan uses both people and circumstances to steal our hope and kill our joy. Placing our highest hope in Jesus

Christ—no one and nothing else—is the only path that does not lead to a disappointing dead end. Everyone and everything else is temporal. People can be fickle; investments can lose value; jobs come and go. Jesus Christ is the same yesterday, today, and tomorrow.

The Bible states that God is no respecter of persons. Neither is Satan. He is an equal opportunity attacker without regard for age, race, sex, religion, or lack of religion. Everyone is a potential target as the enemy sets about furthering his evil agenda.

8 Preparation for the Future

This chapter is primarily devoted to giving due consideration to educational options for your children. However, even more basic and essential than education is their identity—how they see and define themselves. It is a parent's job to carefully craft the parameters in which children make discoveries and learn about themselves.

Their basic identity lies in being a child of God. Children need to be assured often that God was their creator, and He has made no one else exactly like them. (Even identical twins sharing the same DNA have differences.) It is vital for children to know deep down that God made them for a purpose, and He has a marvelous destiny in mind for each one. If every parent instilled this knowledge, there would be little need to teach self-esteem because each child would know that he or she is highly esteemed and valued by the Lord of the universe.

Their next source of identity comes from knowing that they have an important place within their family. No child should feel expendable or that someone else could ever take his or her place. On the other hand, neither should they have the sense that the family revolves around them. The parents are the managers/coaches and they are clearly the ones who should be in charge. It is within a family that the first concepts of teamwork are taught.

It is troubling to see twenty-somethings who are drifting through life, trying to "discover themselves" or "find themselves". The reality is that these young adults never discovered their true identity. Why not? Because they were conforming to their peers or fulfilling parental expectations. Now they are expected to be on their own. Most desire independence, but they've had little practice at being independent. They find themselves at a crossroad where they must choose a direction or take the next step. Without a clear sense of identity, it's difficult to get a clear sense of direction.

The process of discovering individual personalities and God-given gifts needs to begin at an early age and will continue for many years. Helping children make these discoveries is not a difficult task, but it does require parents to be intentional and observant. Even during infancy, you can begin to detect traits that give clues to the makeup of your child.

Since I appreciate predictability, I would try to figure out my firstborn's behavior patterns. Although many of them quickly changed through developmental stages, I noticed as an infant that her happiest days were those when we left the house to go anywhere. As a pre-schooler, the first thing she asked every morning was, "Where are we going today, Mama?"

These were clues to how God wired her. Throughout her life she's liked meeting new people, going new places, and facing new challenges. These are ideal characteristics for what the Lord had planned. She is a military wife, whose life is filled with continual change and challenges of new locales and new friendships.

Remember my baby who had her days and nights mixed up? Yes, she has she remained a night owl, and so is her mate. Her breech birth was unconventional and she chose an unconventional path when she volunteered to teach in a Malawi orphanage before entering college.

Then there is my son whose first word was not "mama" or "dada". It was "ball". If a game is played with a ball, he has always wanted to play—and win! Now a basketball coach, he trains and motivates his team to compete for the win.

Keep in mind that parents should operate as guardians, not owners. Your children belong to the Lord first, and He's entrusted them to you. Kids can gain a better understanding of their identity when parents are willing to transfer *some* power in *some* areas. The trick is to strike a balance. Relinquishing *too* much authority to your children in those early formative years makes recouping it quite difficult when they hit their teens. If your teen has a leader personality, then conflict is inevitable as you keep reminding them who God has put in charge.

Allowing young children to make age-appropriate decisions is a safe way to transfer some power, it gives them valuable practice, and it serves as a legitimate esteem-builder. For example, at a young age all my kids wanted to choose for themselves what clothes to wear for the day. Without boundaries, clothes can become a battleground, so I allowed only acceptable options to be available. In the middle of January there were no sundresses and sandals in their closets—only cold weather clothes. As an "old school" mom, I taught them that on Sundays we dressed up for church and saved our tee shirts and stained pants for playing outside.

Children also like to have a voice in choosing the décor of their room. If two are sharing a room, then there will be a three-way negotiation. Spencer was about eight when I decided that his boring beige bedroom walls needed some color. Knowing his favorite color was green, and being a green lover myself, we had a starting point. I was picturing keeping two walls neutral and the other two hunter green—a masculine look. Spencer's idea was to have all four walls alike and his choice was sea green. To me, sea green didn't say "boy", but that's what we went with, and he was content with that color for years.

"One plan fits all" does not apply to raising children. To successfully enable each child to be all that God intends, we must seek His direction and guidance for each child. Just because a particular tactic worked for child #1 doesn't mean we should use the same tactic for child #2. Our Father is very creative, and therefore we should strive to be creative fathers and mothers as well. If we treat every child exactly the same way, if we apply the same discipline across the board, then we should not be surprised when we reap a rebellious teen.

Speaking of the teen years, God does not want you to dread this period of your child's life. Instead, I believe He wants you to approach that stage with positive expectations. If you *expect* problems and rebellion, problems and rebellion will be what you receive. If you *expect* them to distance themselves from you, that is what will happen.

What you can safely expect is change and more change. Communication patterns may change, and it's the parent who has to adapt. It's *always* the parent who must adapt as the child "tries on" things that are different. That's why my prayer has consistently been "Let me be the mother that Rachel needs me to be, the mother that Julia needs me to be, the mother that Spencer needs me to be." Even when they act like they don't need or want a mother, that's still what my prayer should be.

Educational Paths

Back in the mid-century years of the 1950's and 1960's, elementary and secondary education was not complicated if you were white and lived outside a big city. You may have had two choices— the public schools in your local district or a parochial school. In my town of 23,000, race was scarcely an issue since 99% of African Americans lived in the same part of town and they had their own schools. With the advent of integration, the high school attended only by blacks was closed, and its students were absorbed into the larger population of the only other public high school in town.

Fifty years later, living in a larger metropolitan area causes me to question if somehow I was transported to another planet. For one thing, there are just so many choices: traditional public schools, charter schools, Christian schools, private schools, parochial schools,

Montessorie schools, public schools that are themed, and the list goes on.

Then there's the option of teaching your children at home entirely by yourself or utilizing classes and programs to round out the curriculum. In the expansive world of home education, the possibilities of how to go about it are varied because the idea is to customize a plan for each child or at least each family.

Just the fact that there are all these choices can be overwhelming. Where does one begin?

The single most important thing I want you to take away is this: **If you haven't asked God to show you where your child should attend school, then you won't know.** If you are happy with where your child is attending school right now, then consider that God may have directed your steps *without* your having asked. However, if you are frustrated for any reason about your child's current school, then it's not too late to ask the Lord to give you His plan.

Our family's journey of education has taken us on a long and winding path that includes ten years of private Christian schools, seven years of homeschooling, four years in public school, and four years of Catholic school. How many mothers have a resume to equal that? I can honestly say that there are advantages and disadvantages to each of them, and if I had to do it all again, there is very little I would change.

My husband and I are both products of public education all the way through earning our Bachelor degrees. If I had remained living in the town where I grew up, I would have unquestioningly placed my children on the same path that had served me well.

We moved to Georgia with our baby girl in 1979, and it wasn't long before the newspaper articles about Georgia public education grabbed our attention. Every year the reports were more negative than positive. Based on SAT scores, the state of Georgia consistently held a ranking among the bottom five of the nation. County by county, test scores for individual schools (primary and secondary) were posted, and the majority ranked below national averages. Still, I was not overly concerned because I was assured time and again that we lived in one of the best districts in our county.

For kindergarten, we placed Rachel at the church where she had attended pre-school, but when kindergarten was over, a change would be necessary. I decided that I should check out the local school for myself, meet the principal, and visit the first grade classes. Little did I suspect what an anomaly I must have been.

Before my pre-arranged visit, I prayed, "Lord, if this is not the school where my daughter should go, then let me *see* something or let me *hear* something that would let me know for sure." That was a very specific prayer and God answered very specifically.

In the first classroom I observed the children in centers. One center was about recognizing shapes and their names. On paper that had been laminated, the word "rectangle" was misspelled. The "c" had been omitted. The implications of that error flooded my mind. The teacher either had not noticed her mistake, or she hadn't bothered to correct it. Maybe she was just a poor speller. No matter the reason, as a stickler for spelling, the outcome was not acceptable.

The next class I visited was listening while the teacher read aloud a story. Every time she came to the word "Mrs." in the book, what I heard her say was "Mizrus". What? Never before had I heard such usage. Other than that one word, the teacher spoke American English, and I was clueless why she was mispronouncing it. Only after sharing this incident with a "GRITS" (Girl Raised in the South), did I learn "Mizrus" was common usage in south Georgia and Alabama, particularly among African Americans.

My next stop was the principal's office. The man was obviously proud of his school and his staff, and if there should ever be a point of disagreement between teacher and parent, I knew he would always support the teacher. Mentioning the relatively small errors I had just witnessed would have been futile, so I kept my mouth shut.

Walking quickly across the parking lot, I got into my car and just sat there as tears filled my eyes. I couldn't ignore what God had made so clear, but now I had no idea where my daughter would be going to first grade. My own education regarding schools had just been launched.

For most families to send a child to a private school requires some level of sacrifice. I remember telling the Lord, "If I never get a Mercedes…if I never get another new car, it will be okay."

I want to state right now that neither Jack nor I regret the dollars we've spent on education that go beyond our tax dollars that are earmarked for education. Unlike taxes, paying tuition is a choice. There were times that the amount of funds available did not make it easy to write the checks, but they were written willingly, with the belief that we were investing now and for the future of our children.

During the mid-to-late 1980's, we came to know several families in our church who had made the decision to teach their children at home. Some of these kids were close friends with our kids. I had tremendous respect for these mothers who were making sacrifices beyond the financial ones. To me, they had given up having lives of their own. Of course it is true that to some extent it can be said that every mother gives up having a life of her own because her life is woven with that of her children. However, in my opinion, these home-educator moms carried the motherhood commitment to a different level. Thankfully the Lord had not called *me* to make that commitment because I knew I was not up to it.

In 1993, we had all three children attending a Christian school despite our declining income in recent years. When we found out there would be a sizeable tuition increase for the next school year, we realized there was no way we could swing it. Additionally, we planned to move from our current house, and only the Lord knew exactly where we would be living. It seemed like the best option was to plan to teach the younger two myself and have my high-schooler attend school *somewhere*.

It was difficult to explain all this to the children. As parents we felt like we had really let our kids down.

There was a spring homeschooling workshop that we thought was important to attend. It was organized by a Christian homeschool father named Gregg Harris from Oregon who had devised some practical tools to make the job easier. His eldest son Josh, age twenty, was one of several speakers. Josh shared from his life, past and present. Currently he was publishing a magazine for teens who were doing school at home. Josh had never attended an official school in his life. He was a product of home education. Standing before us, we heard the most "had it all together" twenty-year-old young man we'd ever witnessed. He was poised and articulate as he spoke of his immediate and long-range goals. Most importantly, his heart was set on the Lord and the principles of the Word. If this guy was the result of home education, who wouldn't want their child to grow up the same way!

Immediately Jack began asking why I wasn't going to homeschool Rachel with the other two. Was he crazy? She was entering tenth grade, and didn't he remember how difficult high school courses could be? No way could I teach math or science on that level!

By the end of the conference, I knew in my heart that I had to at least give it prayerful consideration, so I asked Rachel to do the same. I asked her to write down all the pros and cons of doing school at home the next year. I don't recall the specifics of her lists, but both of us could see that the scales tipped heavily in favor of the pros. The few cons were mostly inconsequential. Neither of us was overwhelmed with enthusiasm, but we believed if we trusted the Lord with the outcome, somehow it would be okay.

In that summer before our homeschool adventure began, what surprised me was the reaction of Rachel's friends in our church. I did not expect others to envy my daughter. As mentioned, every teen knew someone who homeschooled, so the practice was more familiar than foreign. All their comments had a common theme.

"I wish my mother would homeschool me." "Rachel, you are so lucky."

Lucky? In my mind, the reason I *had* to homeschool was because

I couldn't afford a private school, and it sure didn't feel like good luck had brought me to that point.

If God is leading you to do something, the outcome will be far better than just okay. He did far more than we imagined. Having her share more responsibility for her education proved to be a very good experience—the type of experience that truly prepares one for college. About six months after starting school at home, I was delighted to hear both girls say how happy they were to be learning at home. Were these the same kids who cried last year at the prospect of not returning to their school?

Rachel made a statement that resonated loudly. She said, "I could have never realized who I was if I had stayed at (name of Christian school)."

Wow. Now I started to understand more fully something I had pondered for a long time. Years before, a mother with older daughters had told me that the peer pressure in a Christian high school was greater than the peer pressure in a public school. At the time, that statement did not make sense to me. Her explanation was that in a small school environment where families hold similar values, there is much pressure for the children to conform and be just like everyone else. In other words, the kids will generally stay within the same comfort zone as their peers.

This has become my opinion as well. Whether we're talking about clothes, cars, or dating, the smaller the peer group and the less diverse that group is, the greater the pressure to fit in.

Let's use transportation as an example. To attend a private school, usually it's left to the family to provide transportation. Often the school does not have buses, but if it does, then that's just another added expense above tuition. As a carpool veteran, I can advise that while some convenience is gained in sharing the driving duties, the tradeoff can be plenty of hassles.

You'll have to look hard to find an American teen who doesn't want their own car just as soon as their license gets printed. Now couple those kids with parents who have tired of being taxi drivers. The solution that makes everyone happy is to buy the student a car in their junior or senior year, if they can afford to do so. In a private school, your child can find himself in the minority without his own set of wheels, whereas in a metro public school, if he rides one of dozens of school buses, he sure doesn't feel like a lone ranger.

Please understand that I am an advocate for public education and private education, as well as home education. There is a place and a need for each one. The key is discovering God's plan for *your* family, *your* child, and as I stated, you won't know what that is unless you take the time to ask, seek, and listen.

Public high schools can be an excellent choice for children who have been given a solid foundation of Biblical principles and have incorporated them into the fabric of their identity. Yes, contrary to public opinion, teenagers who know who they are and what they believe actually exist! On the other hand, public high schools may not be the best choice for those who lack the maturity to go against the tide of public opinion, who are easily swayed, or who are interested in pleasing peers and teachers rather than challenging them.

In a larger public school environment where there are 300-900 per grade, no single student can begin to know everyone. That is not a bad thing. The whole school population is so diverse in terms of ethnicity, religion (or lack thereof), family income, family educational background, etc. that every child can find a group of peers where he or she fits in. Nerds still hang with nerds, jocks hang with jocks, and the pretty, popular people still have their cliques. Through the generations, some social groupings stay the same.

A big advantage offered by most public high schools is the wide variety of extracurriculars that are offered. It is in school clubs where leadership can be fostered in a quiet student. Athletic teams abound on many levels for many sports. The arts are strong—drama, music, dance, creative art. It's like choosing what appeals to you from a smorgasbord. You can taste new things and decide what you really like.

In Rachel's declaration, she was saying she no longer needed to think or act like everyone else thought or acted. She knew she was loved and accepted by those with whom she spent most of her waking hours—family. She now had the time to just **think** and to simply **be.** She wasn't caught up in competition with anyone but herself. All the energy she had spent in comparing herself with her friends was now being used more constructively.

Teaching your children at home makes protection of their minds and spirits a whole lot easier. Prevention of problems is always more effective than trying to devise solutions and fixes after the problems exist. Teaching foundational truths is more difficult when you must un-teach what is being espoused at school. Immediately Darwinism may pop into your head, but in the lower grades it takes a more subtle form. It is nature itself that is revered rather than the One who spoke nature into existence.

Many Christian parents divide family life into three main parts—home, school, and church. If each part can support and reinforce the other two parts, then they fit like puzzle pieces. If one part has an agenda that does not reinforce the other two, then those two have to work harder and unify to overcome the weaknesses of that other part.

There was a church function where I was seated at a table next to a father with two little girls. The older daughter was in first grade and the little one was less than one year. When the dad learned that I was a seasoned home educator, he asked lots of questions, and it quickly became apparent that he had concerns about his daughter's current school experience.

In terms of grades, she seemed to be doing fine. He really didn't know details about what happened daily at school because reports from a six year old are sketchy at best. What he did know was that when his precious child got off the bus every afternoon, she seemed "like a different person than the one who got on the bus in the morning". Parents, that is a red flag! His little girl was more subdued, less joyful. On top of that, she had homework that was taking two hours to complete every evening. The family's schedule was revolving around helping her complete assignments and getting her to bed at a reasonable hour so she could get up early and do it all over again the next day.

In my humble opinion, this should not be the life of a six year old. The dad was disbelieving at first when I told him what was possible if his daughter received her instruction at home. With few interruptions, she could do everything necessary in three to four hours max under the guidance of her mother. They could set their own schedule. She would have time to just play, and the whole family could spend their evenings in a peaceful, relaxed atmosphere with the parents not feeling enslaved to homework! During our conversation the dad also mentioned that it wasn't possible for his wife and him to attend a home group since groups met on school nights. That's a big tradeoff.

I never saw that family again, so I don't know if any changes were ever made. I hope so because if a child is feeling burdened by school in first grade, just imagine how she'll feel by tenth grade. What I saw in Rachel's high school friends was that many of them were experiencing burnout. Some of it came from the relentless pressure of working and competing for the grade. Mentally they were just tired of playing the game and wanted it to be over. Spiritually they had been fighting the good fight in their schools for many years, long before they ever heard the term "spiritual warfare". Now they were battle-weary.

I have alluded to the home education benefit of having greater control over your schedule, and since I've never met a family in opposition to that, everyone can imagine how this would come into play in your own situation. Whether it's working around naps or errands or illness, women who are committed to their children's education will get the job done, and they will do it feeling less stressed. When much of the outside pressure of timetables is eliminated, it actually forces you to be a better steward of the hours in your day.

In a way that nothing else consistently does, educating multiple children at home promotes family unity. Younger children learn from older siblings. Together they can learn history or science, just at different levels. Remember the one-room schoolhouse? There were multiple kids, multiple grade levels, and one teacher to oversee everything. It worked!

The big advantage teacher-moms have today is the wide selection of varied curriculums that are readily available. Today we recognize that not everyone learns the same way. Some prefer learning visually; some people are more auditory and would prefer to listen rather than read. Others learn best through hands-on involvement. You can choose what fits your child's learning style, and of course it's hard to beat the internet when it comes to having a media center at your fingertips.

Jeremiah 29:11 tells us that the Lord knows the plans He has for us, that those plans are for good, and that they include giving us a future. God not only sees the all-encompassing future from now to infinity, but he has designed a future for each one of us. Verse 13 holds the key to discovery. "If you look for me wholeheartedly, you will find me." (NLT)

I encourage everyone to seek God's plan in regard to the education of your children. What is the easy choice today may not prove to be the best choice in the future. Let's be done with big regrets and move forward confidently, trusting God's guidance for those lives He entrusted to you.

9 Dispelling Some Myths

MYTH #1

YOU WILL SPOIL A CHILD IF YOU GIVE THEM TOO MUCH LOVE

Not true unless your definition of love includes giving them lots of *things* or when *things* are supposed to be a replacement for time, attention, and physical contact.

Fifty years ago the prevailing thought was that mothers shouldn't cuddle their babies just to be cuddling because too much of that would "spoil" them. Then the pendulum swung, and "family bed" gained popularity, giving rise to the notion that it's impossible to have too much physical contact.

I'm not going to debate either of these, but I do assert that physical affection and interaction are very important from infancy through the teen years. During the first couple years of life, it is not only essential to the child's overall sense of security, but have you considered what it does for the parents? It strengthens that emotional bond for us, too.

This is why it's vital that dads not be excluded from the picture. Yes, only mothers are endowed with lactating breasts, but early on, a dad's special style of nurturing and care-giving should be encouraged. It's about more than just changing diapers and rocking a fussy baby.

In the interest of sharing the workload, instead of letting Jack retire to the couch to read the newspaper and watch TV following dinner, I'd often ask for his help. He could either give baths to kids or wash dishes. Fortunately for all of us, he chose to be a bath-giver rather than a dish-washer. Every square inch of their little bodies got vigorously scrubbed. They learned water was nothing to fear as they spluttered through repeated dousing to thoroughly rinse the shampoo. Baths served as a father-child bonding experience!

Additional bonding occurred right after the bath. When the girls got old enough to sit safely on the lavatory countertop, that's where Jack would place them after they were towel-dried and in their PJs. Then he'd begin the process of detangling their long hair, and a process it was. They were wiggly, full of "ouches", and eager to be done. However, he patiently combed to smooth every tangle and get the "part" perfectly straight. Watching him take that kind of care was so endearing.

Another huge contribution that dads can make fairly effortlessly is simply to do some roughhousing with the kids. What a fun way to give physical attention! Rolling around on the floor is developmentally a sound practice and will be fondly remembered long after you've put that educational toy in the garage sale.

Besides physical affection, kids also crave verbal affection. This should come in the form of sincere praise and deserved praise. It doesn't take long for kids to detect if we're conning them.

Adults of our grandparents' era didn't give compliments freely because they didn't want a child to get a "big head". Now adults have moved to the other extreme. They gush over anything and everything a child says or does. "That's just so cute." "You're so special."

Surely there is a balance. Catch your kids doing something right and acknowledge it! Thank them helping, for making good choices, for obeying immediately. Praise them for the emerging traits of character you see developing—for honesty, for unselfishness, for loyalty. This is the type of verbal affection that makes an impact.

MYTH #2

THE QUALITY OF TIME SPENT WITH A CHILD IS MORE IMPORTANT THAN THE QUANTITY

Now who do you suppose came up with this concept? A parent who wanted to assuage his guilt for not spending more time with his or her child, that's who!

Who gets to determine what is "quality time" and what isn't? The adult or the child? Are we going to judge quality based simply on the activity itself? What rates higher—bike riding or a game of checkers? Reading a book or having a tea party?

What about ranking activities according to where they take place? Then a museum will trump a park because for sure "educational" experiences are higher quality than simply "playing". Does this sound absurd? Totally!

The primary purpose of spending time with your child is *interaction*. That's not a difficult concept to grasp. Interaction includes lots of dialogue and a shared focus. Whether you are playing "Old Maid" or visiting the zoo, you need to be engaged and giving your attention. If you allow technology to interfere and interrupt, then you are diminishing the quality of interaction.

If you receive calls and send text messages while strolling through the zoo, where has your attention really been? It reminds me of the classic scene with the husband and wife sitting at the breakfast table. The husband's eyes are on his newspaper while the wife is chattering away, and he mutters a few "uh-huh's". Yes, they ate breakfast together, but it is hardly quality time.

Please don't be fooled into thinking that the best times are the ones with the most photo ops. Just because we're parents doesn't make us immune to peer pressure, so buck the crowd and don't succumb to the pressure of having an extravagant birthday party *every* year and inviting *every* kid in the class, or on the team.

My experience has been that quality time often comes in ways that are unscheduled. Car rides home from school can be a time of significant sharing about your child's day. Car rides anywhere can be good as long as radios, iPods, DVD's, etc. are off so that conversation can take place. Bedtime is another opportunity where you and your child can talk one-to-one about whatever is on his or her mind.

The Lord gives us all the same amount of time, the same number of hours in each day. We have choices as to how we'll fill those hours. The wise will make at least a few of those hours count for eternity.

MYTH #3

PARENTS SHOULD TREAT ALL THEIR CHILDREN EXACTLY THE SAME

Showing favoritism to one child over another is certainly folly. It destroys the unity in a family and sets up an unhealthy competition.

Look in Genesis to see what happened to the twins Jacob and Esau when Jacob was favored by his mother Rebekah and Esau was favored by his father Isaac. Rebekah aided her favorite son in deceiving his father, and when Esau discovered the trickery, Jacob had to flee for his life. It was twenty years before the brothers were reconciled.

Yet Jacob repeated his own history rather than learning from it. He made the very same mistake with his own boys. He gave one of them a beautifully distinctive coat that was the envy of the older brothers. You probably know the rest of the story. Jealousy caused them to sell Joseph to Egyptian traders and now another family is torn apart. As a parent,

Jacob felt the heartbreak of loss that his own father experienced, but the pain was worse because he believed his son to be dead.

If the objective should be fairness, not favoritism, then why isn't treating all your children the same a good idea?

What God the Father models for us is that He does **not** treat all *His* children the same. Certainly we are all given the same ground rules. God doesn't make exceptions, and say that a commandment applies to me, but doesn't apply to you. While remaining very consistent, He deals with us on an individual, personal level. How he communicates with me is likely very different than how he communicates with you. It's the same with discipline. He disciplines me in a way that will "hit home" because He knows me so very well.

Likewise, we must communicate and deal with each child in a personalized way. I have already mentioned that my prayers have been that I might be the mother that each child needed me to be. I knew that if I simply parented "by the book", I would fail.

The most effective correction of our children is what works best in bringing about the desired results. For some it might be isolating them temporarily; for others it might be removing toys or loss of a privilege. Sometimes what is most effective relates directly to the violation itself.

I recall an occasion when I was going to bake chocolate chip cookies. I was quite sure that I had half of a twelve ounce bag of Nestle chips, but I searched the kitchen cabinets and came up empty. I even asked my family, because I had not yet learned that questions regarding the whereabouts of *anything* are futile ninety-nine percent of the time.

"Does anybody know what happened to the half package of chocolate chips?" was met with three "I don't knows".

Several weeks later, I was pulling Julia's bed out a bit from the wall. There I discovered a crushed, bright yellow Nestle wrapper. The evidence could mean only one thing, and when confronted, Julia admitted her guilt. Knowing that stealing and lying about it were serious offenses, she was ready to receive her spanking.

Not so fast! Because the offenses were indeed serious, I really wanted her to "get" it. With some divine inspiration, I devised a punishment far more impactful than the corporal type. It truly hurt. For the next two weeks Julia would not be permitted any desserts or candy, and for someone with a sweet tooth, it was pure torture to see ice cream dipped and cookies dispensed for everyone else, knowing she had brought the consequence upon herself.

I am confident that the Lord will direct you in how to parent each child in personal, meaningful ways, designed as uniquely as He created them. As James instructed, "If any of you lacks wisdom, he should ask God, who gives generously to all without finding fault, and it will be given to him." (James 1:5 NIV)

MYTH #4

INDOCTRINATION OF CHILDREN SHOULD BE AVOIDED

Just the word "indoctrination" can paint a mental picture that is harsh and cold if it is narrowly viewed. The word "doctrine" is used multiple times in the New Testament and means instruction or teaching. To "indoctrinate" can mean to instruct in a doctrine or ideology, or more generally, it means to teach.

After sharing so much about my children, what kind of grandmother would I be if I didn't relate at least one incident about my wonderful grandchildren?

We had the three of them in the car going to a pizza restaurant. Stopped at a red light, Andrew, age eight, spoke soberly. "There's a bad sign on that car."

My eyes quickly searched for profanity or obscene messages on bumper stickers, but seeing nothing offensive, I hesitated to push for more information.

However, Andrew next pointed out the bad sign to his sister who quickly agreed with his assessment, so I turned around to look out the rear passenger window. Then I saw it. There was a magnetic sign on the rear door of an adjacent vehicle. Stark in its simplicity, about fifteen inches tall, was a red capital "G" on a black background.

For you non-Georgians, this symbolizes the University of Georgia just as surely as their bulldog mascot. I had to laugh as I immediately understood why this sign was "bad". Their dad (my son-in-law) was a proud graduate of the Georgia Institute of Technology, and he had clearly been indoctrinating impressionable minds. No doubt a big "GT" or yellow jacket sign would have garnered positive comments.

Everyone has biases about *something*. Unless you are that singular person with absolutely *no preferences and no convictions*, then you are biased. Some people are very vocal about their biases, while others keep their biased opinions to themselves. Biases may be pro or con.

I admit that I am biased against yellow cars and yellow houses, and never would I buy either one. Some folks are very biased toward one automaker and would never consider purchasing anything else. Biases are not intrinsically bad or wrong, and my two examples are harmless and trivial in the scope of life.

One of my serious "biases" is that the Holy Bible is the inspired, infallible Word of God. I believe it is the ultimate reference for life and superior to all other religious books and writings. This is what I taught my children, and this is what they grew up believing unquestioningly.

You see where I'm going with this. It is a parent's *duty* to "indoctrinate" their kids when it comes to values and belief systems. Do you want their framework for life to be built by you, or will you permit it to be built by their peers or teachers? Maybe the greatest foolishness is to allow children to sort out everything for themselves. Yet today's trend is to expose children to many avenues and allow them to choose.

Health-conscious parents don't set out the cupcakes with the meat and vegetables because they know which has the greater appeal. Unless you teach/indoctrinate them about which foods you consider "junk", then you are setting them up for an unhealthy lifestyle.

In the Old Testament no one questioned the fact that God-fearing parents should instruct their children in the ways of the Lord. The book of Proverbs is filled with numerous admonitions to sons to heed the teaching of their fathers.

"Listen, my sons, to a father's instruction; pay attention and gain understanding. I give you sound learning, so do not forsake my teaching." (Prov. 4:1–2 NIV)

"Listen, my son, accept what I say, and the years of your life will be many. I guide you in the way of wisdom and lead you along straight paths." (Prov. 4:10–11 NIV) Then again in verses 20–22 the father admonishes his son to listen closely to his words, keeping them within his heart, for they will bring life and health to the whole body.

After giving Moses the Ten Commandments, the Lord made it clear what His people were to do. "Impress them on your children. Talk about them when you sit at home and when you walk along the road, when you lie down and when you get up." (Deut. 6:7 NIV)

In light of scriptural admonitions too numerous to list, how can we *not* be very intentional when it comes to instructing our children what we believe about Jesus Christ and His church, and why we believe it? Why not go a step further and explain why you do *not* place your faith in other religious belief systems?

Political correctness appears to foster timidity in Christians, but it promotes boldness in other religions that also have the goal of taking their message to the whole world. I'm thinking specifically of Muslims, and I'm not afraid to say so.

The Muslim religion is doing an excellent job when it comes to indoctrinating their children. I overheard a second grade girl tell her classmate that only Muslims would be in heaven; everyone else would be in hell. The other kid looked a bit surprised at this news, but he didn't say anything.

This same girl proudly goes to school on Muslim religious holidays dressed in her finest outfits. Her hands are decorated with elaborate ink drawings, and she is not embarrassed to answer the questions of other students. Just her ability to answer their questions lets me know that her parents have not shirked their duty. In her quiet way, Sana lets her world see her religion.

Outside the United States, Muslim parents raise the level of indoctrination to a higher bar. They teach their children that their religious beliefs must be defended, even to the point of death. Martyrdom is not to be feared, but welcomed. The Western mindset cannot comprehend a culture where one family member blesses another family member's decision to wear a suicide bomb for the purpose of making a religious or political statement.

As Christians how do we dare keep silent? How can we fail to inform children of the martyrs of our own faith? I don't mean just the martyrs in the New Testament or those in the time of Joan of Arc. Christian martyrdom is happening *now*. Currently in parts of Asia and Africa people are tortured and killed because they have embraced Jesus Christ, the Holy One who laid down His life for them.

In Luke 12 Jesus states that whoever denies him before men will be denied before the angels. That's a powerful warning. Most denials are not given in a loud, clear voice. The strongest denials occur when we keep our mouths shut rather than speaking the truth.

And you're reluctant to indoctrinate your kids? Personally, I'm afraid not to! I see repercussions while on this earth and furthermore, I don't want it held to my account on Judgment Day. It seems to me that the wise, no-regret choice is to write my cherished beliefs upon the slates of my children's minds. In fact, it is my duty as a guardian.

Wrapping it up

Solomon wrote in Psalm 127(NLT) that children are a gift from the Lord, a reward. He next proclaims that children are like arrows in a warrior's hands, and joyful (blessed) is he whose quiver is full of them.

Since it is recorded in 1 Kings 11 that Solomon had 700 wives, I'm guessing he had dozens of full quivers!

Certainly it requires strength—physical, emotional, and spiritual strength— to take those arrows from the Lord and fashion them into weapons. At times your energy will be depleted, and you will question how long you can last when running on fumes. That's the precise time when God steps in, for *His* strength is perfected in *your* weakness. He wants to fill your empty tank with Himself.

"Let's not get tired of doing what is good. At just the right time we will reap a harvest of blessing if we don't give up." (Gal. 6:9 NLT) What might that harvest of blessing look like?

Based on Paul's instructions to the Colossians in chapter 2:7–8 (NLT), I desire that my harvest of blessing—my children—be firmly rooted in Jesus Christ so that their lives will be built on Him. I am expecting their faith to be strong enough so that they will not be captured "with empty philosophies and high-sounding nonsense that come from human thinking and from the spiritual powers of this world, rather than from Christ."

It is my sincere hope that my children think they have been endowed with a rich spiritual legacy. Not only have they been my good and perfect gifts, they are my best gifts to the world. They are people who will make a difference for the Kingdom. In truth, they already have, and I am confident that the spiritual legacies to their own children will be even richer and fuller.

Let the Word of the Lord continually give you encouragement and hope. "If God is for us, who can ever be against us? Since he did not spare even his own Son but gave him up for us all, won't he also give us everything else?" (Rom. 8:31–32 NLT) Truly He has provided all of us with the tools we need to fulfill our callings as guardian parents.